BEVERAGES OF OAXACA

SALVADOR CUEVA
& RICARDO BONILLA

BEVERAGES OF OAXACA

Salvador Cueva / Ricardo Bonilla
Text: Salvador Hernández Cueva / Ricardo Bonilla Cazarín
Editor: Cuauhtémoc Peña
Photography: Salvador Hernández Cueva
English translation: Isabel Torrealba
Proof reading: Ricardo Bonilla Cazarín
Graphic design: Moisés Guillén
Illustrations: Moisés Guillén / Indira Cevallos
Pre-press and color correction: Manuel García Díaz
Printed by: Repro.Gráfika, S.C.
Editorial Agua de Tiempo
ISBN (hardcover): 978-1-647-13997-1
ISBN (softcover): 978-1-647-64683-7

1a. Edition, Oaxaca, México. January, 2020

They say that in Oaxaca one drinks their coffee with mezcal…
The say that in Oaxaca hot chocolate is prepared with water…
"Cumbia del mole" *(La Cantina, 2006)*
Lila Downs

INDEX

Acknowledgements

This work wouldn't have been possible without several people who came together. Many of them are, in truth, the protagonists of this work: the traditional cooks, who are heirs of their culture, legacy of their community and of the numerous towns that form what we have come to know today as Oaxaca, a place which represents unity and diversity. We thank each and every single one of them, but also those who gave us their support in one way or another. Particularly, the authors of this work want to extend our gratitude to: Marycarmen Vázquez and her family, Sandra Vázquez Fernández, Leticia Tamayo Rodríguez, Eduardo González Reyes, Elvia Patricia Castillejos López, Francisco and Gabriel Ríos along with their family, Huatulco's El Grillo Marinero restaurant, Edith Bustillo Cacho, Libia Cortés Bustillo, Judith Juárez Sánchez, Salvador López Toledo, Rafael Mier, Café Huatulco, The Mexican Corn Tortilla Foundation, Rosita Ramos, Pedro López Merino, Aimee Chávez and her family, Erik León, Víctor Cruz, Elizabeth Hernández, Leticia Santiago, Verónica and Nuvi Coronel Sánchez, Moctezuma Zurita, Ignacio López Calvo, Rebeca Cruz, Bibiana Bautista Gaytán, The Milenary Women Organization, Valentín Arellanes and his family, Luis Ángel Leodegario, Rosaura Duarte Reyes, Moisés Quiroz, Jorge Enrique Gutiérrez Sámano, Luisa Esther Montalvo Martínez, Joel Merino, Amado Néstor Hernández Torres, Miguelina Torres Salinas, Martha Jimenez, Andrés Portela, Pablo Raña, Wilfrido Santiago Marcial, Adriana Aguilar Escobar, SECULTA, Marcela Flores Iga, Laura Ileana Ibarra Schaufelberger, Amairani Márquez, Carmen Molina Olivares, Mayela García, Maribel Campos Muñuzuri, Gaby Villa Mayoral, Yesica Silva, Carla López, Fuica Ambrosio, Luis Sosa, María Alaz, Edwin Lara, Sher Alvarado, Beno Ramírez, Rafael Mier, Mildred Daniel, Lorena Terán, Omar Alonso, Joseph Gilbert, Elízabeth Hernández, Alex Jandernoa, Ramsés Ruíz, Francisco Musi, and Fernando Cervantes.

We are also grateful to the company Anfora for the gifts they provided for those who shared their beverages with us.

We would especially like to thank the following people who did tremendous work in their respective regions by reaching out to others, getting involved, and thoroughly documenting several beverages. Particularly to Cibeles Ramírez Colmenares, for being the first person who trusted us when we first arrived to Oaxaca, for opening the very first door, for accompanying us through documenting many beverages, for her attentiveness, love, and continuous promotion of this project. For her support when our travel resources were running out. Thank you so much for making this project yours, and for treating us as if we were your own family.

To Celia Florián, President of the Traditional Cooks of Oaxaca Organization.

Thanks for sharing your contacts with us, for showing the project to the cooks, for documenting beverages with them, for promoting the book, and for your attentiveness while we were on this journey.

To Ixchel Ornelas Hernández for her involvement in the Mixtec region, for showcasing the beverages that many are unaware of, for promoting the project, for teaching us about her region's coffee, for graciously hosting us at her restaurant El Patio in Tlaxiaco.

To Rogelio Chávez from Putla for all his support while we were documenting the beverages from the Sierra Sur, for getting involved and doing everything he could to ensure people in his community were a part of the book, for being a culinary spokesman for the region. Thank you so much for your generosity while we were at your restaurant, Tito's Tierra de Humo, in Putla.

We would also like to especially thank the following people for believing in the project, pushing it forward, and allowing it to become concrete and tangible. Many thanks to Alexandra Cosio and to Juan Carlos Rojas for all their support during this trip, the first of many. Thanks for your trust, for making this project your own for your diligence and facilitating the team that helped make the documenting process go as smoothly as possible. Thanks to our allies at Casa Cuubi in San Antonino Castillo Velasco. We are happy we could team-up and form an alliance so this Beverages of Oaxaca project can be extended into your cultural space through exhibitions and workshops related to beverages, foods, crafts and arts of Oaxaca and its 16 indigenous communities.

Preface

This book is the product of an idea and a personal project of Salvador Cueva who, while traveling outside of Mexico, decided to return and get to know his own country better through photography. However this project was more than just a personal goal. Salvador´s objective was to contribute something meaningful and share what he had learned from the journey.

While looking for the way to do this, he met Ricardo Bonilla, researcher and culinary critic, who understood the importance and strength of the subject matter. He made a commitment to work with him, just as long as it could be true team work, where he could bring depth and vision to the subject, making it so the project could also lead to future culinary research.

At the beginning, the idea was to document the process and preparation of traditional beverages from all over Mexico. For three months, Salvador researched beverages from each state, creating a list and a schedule for their documentation. The vision was to cover seven states during an eighteen-month period. With personal resources, savings, and work, Salvador started his trip to Oaxaca with a list of thirteen beverages he wanted to document. Ricardo set these specific research boundaries and proposed starting just with Oaxaca, as he knew Salvador would find many more beverages that he could have anticipate in this state.

On July 14th, 2018, Salvador began the trip on his own. Since it was the month for The Guelaguetza celebrations, locals were focused on the festivities, making initial contact and work complicated. Even with these initial difficulties, his objectives were clear and he was insistent until someone gave him an opportunity. Through friends, contacts, blog posts, and sharing beverage information via social media, many people became familiar with the project and documenting started to become much easier. During this stage, Ricardo gave important advice, more certain than ever that Salvador could move forward with such a complicated undertaking.

As Salvador travelled and documented, the list kept growing until he realized there was enough material for the book to focus solely on Oaxaca. One day, Salvador heard that, "Oaxaca is a country inside of Mexico." After thirteen months of travel he could confirm that indeed it is. "Oaxaca captivated me because of its people, its biodiversity —in the broadest sense of the word— and the various microclimates that make its gastronomic richness as vast as the range of its mountains," said Salvador, as he continued his venture.

"They did tell me upon my arrival that if 'you eat chapulines, drink *tejate*, and *mezcal*, you will never leave.' I could not be more grateful and in love with the people of Oaxaca, who are the most welcoming I've ever met. They make you part of their family and their group of friends. The first thing they ask when you get to any town, at any time, is, 'have you eaten? Would you like something to drink?' And then, on the table, a story begins," said Salvador. Ricardo saw the work growing with beverages and realized through Salvador's dedication and will they would reach the finish line. He also noticed that, because of his lack of expertise as a culinary researcher and his scarcity of gastronomic knowledge, he could look differently at things that others who had a certain "workshop blindness" and "pride" couldn't, which, in truth, added richness

to the work. And thus a natural union was born between Ricardo, and Salvador's innate curiosity for way of investigating coupled with his talent, discipline, and consistency helped him to collect vital information on the subject. The enriching dialogue between the two always created the best content and results. Even though Salvador began this project on his own, this book you hold in your hands was possible thanks to the many people involved. Teamwork has strengthened this project, providing richer content and extending its reach. "Thanks to all the people who trusted me enough to let me into their home's kitchens," said Salvador when he reached the last stage of the book. "Thanks for allowing me to participate in your dream and for reigniting my belief that young people are trustworthy, that their word means something, and that they can be unwavering when it comes to their proposals. The merit is truly yours," said Ricardo, who not only recognizes Salvador's effort, but also his enormous bravery, passion, and commitment to uphold his dream.

Salvador Cueva and Ricardo Bonilla

Prologue

Beverages accompany foods during any time of day and under different circumstances: everyday meals, ceremonial meals, ritual meals, and those shared during community celebrations.

This book attempts to approach them from an experiential perspective. Photographer Slavador Cueva travelled, talked to the guardians of this traditional knowledge, listened to their stories, photographed them, and established friendship with them. Culinary researcher Ricardo Bonilla wrote complimentary texts to accompany the wide variety of traditional alcoholic and non-alcoholic beverages from the state of Oaxaca.

In order to give the images and accompanying text some context, the authors decided to divide the beverages into the 8 geographical and cultural regions of Oaxaca. Yet, many of them go outside these limits and can be found in markets, food establishments, and family homes no matter their place of origin.

Without a doubt, the environmental and cultural richness of the state explains why the display of gastronomic heritage can come from numerous sources, be prepared with different techniques, and can be consumed during various moments of Oaxacan's lives.

Several of these beverages also have a Pre-Hispanic past and others are the result of cultures coming together through hundreds of years. Fruits, seeds, rinds, leafs, sap, flowers, crusts, stems are among the produce that are either native or of recent occurrence. Raw, roasted, cooked, fermented, distilled, boiled, ground, mixed by mortar and pestle, foamed, cold or hot —each technique with its own specific purpose. From a refreshing *té limón* to a ceremonial *coyul pozol* to a *pataxte atole* for Day of the Dead; a glass of sugarcane *aguardiente* with fruits, herbs or on its own; an *atole, tepache, chileatole,* hot chocolate with water, *café de olla, pozole, tejate, popo, bu'pu, pinole, horchata* with prickly pear, rum, fruit liqueurs, *pulque, curados, mezcal,* or *aguas frescas*— all these beverages have a specific time and place.

The tradition of consuming these beverages is a combination of knowledge that starts with gathering, farming, or shopping for produce; the respective sweeteners and thickeners used; the different preparation methods and ways of serving; the tools and utensils employed, such as tablecloths, napkins, mugs, glasses, drinking gourds, and cups are all parts of the tradition.

We cannot overlook the fact that many of these beverages are exclusively prepared as a community for festivities or religious ceremonies, during family events, as part of a ritual, simply to accompany daily foods, or as a way to quench one's thirst.

When recounting their own stories, the bearers of these traditions portray a world full of myths, legends, fables, community teamwork such as *tequio*, medicinal uses of the spiritual drinks, elixirs and dyes, the ways in which they learned to prepare these beverages, as well as other elements of their region's culture, whether indigenous or mixed, from the city or the countryside.

This is not a recipe book, nor an academic research, but a book that takes us on a journey through many of Oaxaca's towns in order to show us its environmental and cultural richness, its farming and cooking techniques, the people's cultural processes that differentiate them and that they speak of with great pride, which are deeply embedded in the customs and traditions of their communities.

Sol Rubín de la Borbolla

Sierra Sur

This region of Oaxaca borders with five of the eight regions of the state. To the north with the Mixteca, Central Valleys and Sierra Norte; to the south with the Coast; to the east with the Isthmus of Tehuantepec and, finally, to the west with the state of Guerrero. It extends over an enormous area of land that expands through almost all of Oaxaca in a wide corridor of humid ecosystems. It consists of four districts: Miahuatlán, Putla, Sola de Vega, and Yautepec. As the name implies, it is a mountainous area to the south of the Central Valleys that is cut across by the Sierra Madre del Sur.

This area has generally humid climate, as well as microclimates that support the growth of tropical and subtropical plants. Its endemic flora is vast given the paradise-like qualities of the region. Thousands of years ago many people and various communities realized the benefits of this type of climate, leading them to grow several important plants that have become an essential part of their culture and culinary traditions.

Today, the local population includes Zapotecs, Mixes, Tacuates, Mixtecos, Chatinos, Chontales, Amuzgos, Triquis and mestizos whose —as in other areas of Oaxaca— main institution is the nuclear family. Yet, in the highlands, it also includes extended family, further securing the intake of local foods and beverages, many of which have pre-Hispanic origins that go back to the first civilizations that populated the continent.

01

Agua de
moringa

The moringa or drumstick tree can grow to be up to 26 feet high. Its flowers are fragrant and of a white or cream color, contrasting against its green tripinnate leaves made up of many small leaflets. Its leaves, flowers, bark, and pods are edible, as well as its seeds and roots. If you walk along the streets of Putla Villa de Guerrero and of certain towns along the Oaxacan Coast, you would easily spot these beautiful trees. Its scientific name is *Moringa Oleifera*, a tree originating from the south of the Himalayas and northwest of India. There, these trees came to be known as ben *(bān)* and its cultivation soon spread to the Malay Peninsula, where the local population named it moringa *(muringa)*. Merchants then brought it to the Philippines and, many years after, Filipino traders took it to Acapulco and throughout the Pacific Coast of Mexico. This is the reason why moringa can be found from the south of Sonora to Chiapas and even in the southern part of the Baja California Peninsula. In Mexico its gained popularity prepared as tea because of its medicinal properties. The tree is grown extensively in Putla as many believe it can, among other things, prevent diabetes and help level blood glucose.

Rogelio Chávez García

It is also not uncommon to see locals there leaving moringa seeds to dry out in their backyards as it is thought in the are that it can cure cancer. This is why, on Sundays, day of the plaza in Putla, there are medicinal stands selling them. As its scientific name implies, the tree contains an oil *(oleifera)* inside its seeds, which are highly medicinal, although moringa is mainly consumed for its high nutritional value as its considered to be a superfood. Genetic and environmental factors as well as cultivation methods can amplify these characteristics. It is often used to fight malnourishment. In Putla, visitors and guests are often gifted leaves so they can prepare *agua fresca*. Rogelio Chávez, "Roy," says that, "Moringa can be prepared into a tea or *agua fresca*; it's a tree that blooms year-round."

14

Freshly-cut leaves are first washed and disinfected, then all veins are removed to leave only a flat sheet that is then ground in a *metate*. Water is slowly added along with more of the cleaned leaves until a green liquid is obtained. This liquid is then strained through a cheesecloth, decanting all the sediment. The resulting extract is often enhanced with lime, though that addition can be omitted. Moringa flowers have pods with many seeds. When eaten, the seeds' flavor changes from bitter to sweet. Roy says that, "when it's tender you can cook it along with vegetables, *a la Mexicana* (a preparation based on tomatoes, onion, and *chiles*), and also scrambled with eggs." Fresh moringa water can be enjoyed in Putla at Tito's Tierra del Humo restaurant, which Rogelio Chávez García owns. Drank alongside a plate of langoustines in a *chicatana* (flying ants) salsa results in a delicious combination.

Hilda Figueroa García

02
Compuesto
de piña horneada

The pineapple is a fruit originating in South America. It is emblematic in Oaxaca, as it is ubiquitous in the region's food and drinks, which include this González Figueroa family creation that has brought fame to El Sesteadero, a town within the Putla Villa de Guerrero municipality. *Compuestos, preparados,* or *curados* are strong alcoholic beverages made from fresh fruits that are soused in *aguardiente* (generic term for a distilled liquor) and left to rest. They are enjoyed year-round, though particularly during Carnival, as it livens festivities and is widely enjoyed. In Putla, Mrs. Hilda Figueroa García, who comes from Santa María Zacatepec, has been making fruit *compuestos* for eight years, using *aguardiente* that her husband, Mr. Jesús González Rosas, distills himself.

The González Figueroa family prepares *compuestos* from nanche (a small, yellow tropical fruit of the locustberry higher classification), guanábana (soursop), capulín (a wild, black, Mexican cherry), coconut, pineapple, piñuela (the fruit from a type of Bromelia plant), passion fruit, and any other seasonal fruits found in the region. Almost all *compuestos* are prepared in a similar manner, only the pineapple *compuesto* has an extra step, as the fruit is briefly roasted in a bread oven, adding a delicious and distinctive flavor to the drink. "We know this delicious *aguardiente* drink as native or hill pineapple," explains Mrs. Hilda.

First, you cut the whole pineapple into small pieces, including the rind, which are then placed on a baking sheet and roasted, later to be soaked in the distilled liquor or *aguardiente*.

Hilda brings the luscious pineapple to her neighbors, who are bakers. They let her roast the fruit. She places the pineapple inside once the oven starts cooling down, otherwise it can get scorched. "It's slow-roasted," she explains. Three hours later, it's ready. Then, it is placed inside a large, glass container and covered with Mr. Jesús' *aguardiente.* The concoction is left to rest for two months, long enough for the liquid to be "at its prime"; differing from other fruits, which take much longer to become properly macerated. The resulting beverage is dark in color and has a sweet taste of roasted pineapple that can be enjoyed any time of day.

For this reason, El Sesteadero has this and other *compuestos* year-round, for those whom wish to enjoy the Putla delicacy, served cold and on its own.

Rogelio Chávez García

03

Té limón

One of the plants that were brought to Mexico from Asia was lemongrass, locally known as *té limón*. It travelled along with the Manila Galleons several centuries ago and became domesticated for its medicinal properties and to prepare an aromatic beverage that is still consumed in the tropical and subtropical areas where it initially arrived, including Oaxaca. This plant, native to the regions extending from India and Sri Lanka to Southeast Asia, was lauded by local botanists of various communities throughout the Pacific coast, from where it spread towards central, south, and southeast Mexico, reaching even northern parts of the country. In Oaxaca, it grows in the warmer areas and in such large quantities that it even reproduces as a wild grass. Since it is so fragrant, it is not uncommon to find lemongrass in people's backyards. It is considered a relaxing tea, to "reduce anxiety" or as an "everyday water," and it is consumed room temperature, cold, or warm. "It is healthy, organic, easily found in the fields, you go and cut it fresh and naturally, no chemicals, it is delicious," says Rogelio Chávez García, a traditional cook from Putla Villa de Guerrero, who frequently makes it.

This plant, reminiscent of the smell of lime, from which it gets its name, is prepared as a tea, which is also how warm beverages made from flowers, herbs, barks, and all plants in general are known in Mexico. Roy rolls the elongated plant leaves and places them in water inside a drinking gourd.

Then, he boils some water and submerges the leaves for up to five minutes, until they release their flavor. He then removes it from the heat. "Many people grow lemongrass in their homes and you can always find it at the market," he says as he pours a cup of lemongrass tea, which tends to be sweetened with sugar.

Roy has become a great friend of ours while on our journey to document the beverages of Oaxaca. In addition to dedicating his life to traditional cooking thanks to his mother's teachings, from whom he inherited the restaurant Tito's Tierra del Humo, he currently also promotes his cuisine using ingredients solely from the region.

Viviana Natividad López López

04

Tepache de caña

In Mexico, the word *tepache* generally refers to a sweet, pleasant, and refreshing fermented beverage, made from pineapple rinds. However, there are many other fermented beverages bearing this name. During pre-Hispanic times, *tepache* was made from corn, and the term originates from the Nahuatl word *tepiatl*: from the combination of *tepitl*, "tender corn," and *atl*, "water." In Oaxaca there are several types of *tepache*, but in the town of Zafra, within the Putla Villa de Guerrero municipality, it is prepared with sugarcane. Sugarcane is a plant native to Papua New Guinea that was domesticated in the 16th Century when the Spaniards brought it from the Canary Islands to the Caribbean. It came to Mexico along with Hernán Cortés, Marquis of the Oaxacan Valley, who introduced it to the area during the conquest.

Viviana Natividad López López has been using sugarcane to make *tepache* for ten years. She used to only sell the peeled and cleaned sugarcane in plastic bags, which she would discard once the fruit started fermenting, until learning how to make the beverage.

Viviana recalls how she discovered she could make sugarcane *tepache*, "One time I had about six bags left and I thought, 'God, so much waste!' Then I opened the bags and it smelled a tad fermented, which got me thinking maybe I could make *tepache* with them. I threw the sugarcane in a container, added some *panela* (raw sugar), filled it with water and left it to rest. One day, after a month had gone by, my dad asked if I was still using the container. I opened it and found it indeed smelled like *tepache*."

Now, when preparing the *tepache*, Viviana first chooses and buys the sugarcane. Then, she peels and cuts them into small pieces that are then placed into a large clay pot filled with water and a little bit of *piloncillo* (raw sugar), which she then tightly closes as to not let any air or dust in. It is left to ferment for a month.

Once the sugarcane *tepache* is ready, it is served in clay pitchers with ice, lime, and *chile*, adding a refreshing and unique taste to the beverage.

Jovita López Cruz

05

chileatole
rojo

This red *chileatole* from Unión Nacional Zafra, also in the municipality of Putla, has the red tint that is popularly found in the central, southern, and southeastern kitchens of Mexico. It is one of the many varieties of *chileatole* that exist today. The name *chileatole* comes from the marriage between the words *chile* and *atole*. *Atole* is itself derived from the Nahuatl words *atl*, "water," and *ollin*, "movement;" that is, "water that moves" or "water that gives energy." Meanwhile, *chile* comes from *chilli*, a generic term that refers to chili plants. As such, this drink could be said to mean "energizing chili water." Anthropologically speaking, due to its color, this beverage could have had a ritual purpose, as this tone tends to be used in ceremonies. Thus, it is not surprising that this *chileatole* is prepared for weddings, birthdays, or baptisms today. Jovita López Cruz prepares a *chileatole* that parts from that culinary culture that has been practiced and transmitted orally since before recorded history. Jovita mentions that she, "learned to make it when I was fifteen."

My mom taught me. My dad would have to chop a whole sack of corn so we could make a large pot of *chileatole*. And, since there were many of us living at home we had to make enough for my grandma, aunt, and the rest of the family." The corn is first chosen from the family's own cornfield and cleaned to remove all corn silk before being chopped. Then they are brought to a boil in a large pot with a pinch of salt. At once, guajillo and costeño *chiles* are ground in a *metate* with some garlic to form a paste. Some corn kernels that have been reserved are ground into the paste. This grinding process is so labor-intensive it takes almost all day. Water is added to the resulting paste to achieve the reddish liquid that's so essential to the beverage. Meanwhile, once the corn is cooked through, cinnamon, *piloncillo* (raw sugar), and a little *epazote* are added, giving the drink a delicious taste and smell. When the *piloncillo* is whole, it can stick to the pot, so it's important to stir with a wooden spoon continuously, which will also thicken the liquid. Finally, the ground reddish liquid is added to the corn. "There's always *chileatole* here," says Jovita. "They sell it off the road all year long since corn is always grown," she adds while offering us a carved drinking gourd filled with the beverage, beautiful white corn floating on top. The hot drink evokes times of yesteryear.

Simona López Aguilar

06

Atole de mango

As previously mentioned, the word *atole* comes from the Nahuatl *atolli. Atl,* meaning "water," and *tolli,* a noun deriving from the Spanish *todo,* "all," participle of *toloa.* Yet, this verb has a variety of meanings and it is complicated to choose the most appropriate root. There are many types of *atole,* the most popular is one made from cornstarch diluted in water, white in color and of a thick consistency, that is enjoyed for breakfast alongside a tasty tamale. This type of *atole,* generally sweetened with sugar, is the foundation for several *atoles* that are made with various fruits, spices, cereals, and so on. However, mango *atole* breaks apart from the established paradigm of the classic pre-Hispanic *atolli.* First, because mangoes are not endemic to Mexico, instead coming from the

Philippines. Second, the technique used to prepare this beverage differs greatly from the versions made with cornstarch —an ingredient it dispenses with. Simona López Aguilar, a native of Santa María Zacatepec, has been making mango *atole* for over three decades. "My mother would show me and I slowly learned. One day I made it on my own and it came out well," recalls Simona.

Mango *atole* is made using heirloom mangoes harvested in the village between February and April. The mangoes are picked and then peeled, a process that requires a great deal of patience since, depending on the amount of fruits, it can take up to two hours.

Usually, Simona uses about fifty mangoes, though sometimes people place much larger orders and then she'll use around a hundred. "In that case we use a large tub since that amount won't fit inside a pot. I get these larger orders from people having gatherings or celebrations," she says. Once the mangoes have been peeled and cut, they go inside of a clay pot filled with water and then placed over the fire to boil. Simona makes everything in her traditional kitchen. There, she uses two concrete blocks on each side of a pile of firewood to place the pot. Once the water starts bubbling around the mangoes, they get taken-off the pot, water's discarded, and they are soaked again in a mix of water and raw sugar. The amount of sugar will depend on the mangoes' bitterness.

The pot goes back over the heat and Simona continuously stirs the *atole* to prevent it from sticking and spilling its foam. Once the water boils, the pot is removed from heat and allowed to cool. Boiling will change the liquid's color, turning dark brown from the raw sugar. At this point, the mangoes will be falling apart, the raw sugar dissolved, and it should be passed through a strainer.

Mango *atole* can be enjoyed cold or hot, preferably served in a *jícara* (drinking gourd). The prime time to prepare the beverage is between the months of January and April. Like Simona, there are many more *atoleras (atole makers)* who make this traditional drink and sell it in downtown Zacatepec.

07

Compuesto de nanche

Compuestos are commonly prepared in Putla Villa de Guerrero —beverages made from infusing cane sugar liquors with fresh fruits. They can be made with passion fruit, tamarind, piñuela (the fruit from a type of Bromelia plant), sour guava, pineapple, capulín (a wild, black, Mexican cherry), nanche (a small, yellow tropical fruit of the locustberry higher classification), and guanábana (soursop), among other regional fruits. About 160 feet from the Yutee river bridge is Doña Concha, a business that started selling *compuestos* in 1999. They made all sorts of *compuestos* there. Today, Antonia Mejía Camacho, or Toña, the current business owner, is in charge of making them. Mrs. Toña, a Putla native, learned to make *compuestos* eighteen years ago. "My grandmother, my father's mother, started out making *tepache* and pineapple *compuestos*. So did my sister, whose name was Concha, which is where the business' name comes from," she explains.

Antonia Mejía Camacho

The process for making *compuestos* is almost always the same, with the exception of nanche —tasty and uncommon. "I started out small, making two liters of each fruit, and then I made more of the ones people liked best," says Toña, who makes more than thirty flavors today. When nanches —a small, aromatic regional fruit— are ripe, they fall from the trees. When in season, one can find a beautiful yellow carpet of fruits under each tree. Once enough nanches have fallen off, they are picked-up and washed to remove any dirt they might have. Usually, the fruits are placed on baking sheets and left outside in the courtyard to dry under the sun. The drying process will vary depending on weather but it usually takes "eight suns" to fully dry.

The color, texture, and size of the nanches changes under each day's sun. Once dried, the nanches are placed in pots, covered with sugar cane liquor, and tightly closed to avoid letting air or dirt in. After a few days, the nanches will have absorbed the liquor. It is one of the fruits that more quickly absorbs alcohol, so new liquor must be frequently added. Nanches are left to rest in the liquid for a year, which results in a beverage of incomparable taste. After this time, a bit of sugar is added if the fruits weren't sufficiently sweet on their own, though Mrs. Toña offers sugar-free *curados* as well. This beverage can be enjoyed year-round, but Carnival is the ideal time for it.

08

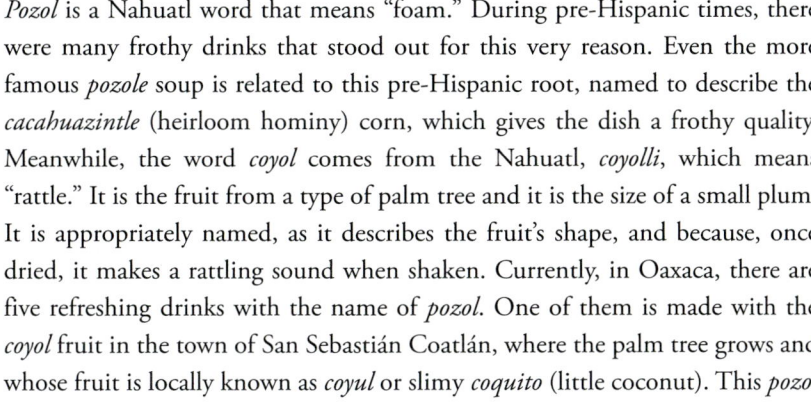

Pozol de
coyul

Pozol is a Nahuatl word that means "foam." During pre-Hispanic times, there were many frothy drinks that stood out for this very reason. Even the more famous *pozole* soup is related to this pre-Hispanic root, named to describe the *cacahuazintle* (heirloom hominy) corn, which gives the dish a frothy quality. Meanwhile, the word *coyol* comes from the Nahuatl, *coyolli*, which means "rattle." It is the fruit from a type of palm tree and it is the size of a small plum. It is appropriately named, as it describes the fruit's shape, and because, once dried, it makes a rattling sound when shaken. Currently, in Oaxaca, there are five refreshing drinks with the name of *pozol*. One of them is made with the *coyol* fruit in the town of San Sebastián Coatlán, where the palm tree grows and whose fruit is locally known as *coyul* or slimy *coquito* (little coconut). This *pozol* is made with nixtamalized corn and *coyol*. "It is prepared for the San Sebastián festival, who is the town's patron saint. It used to be more common, but the boys today don't want to drink it as they prefer other things; they are not as fond of traditional foods," says Petra Valencia, a traditional cook and a native of Miahuatlán, a municipality neighboring the town of San Sebastián Coatlán. *Pozol* is a celebratory drink, but it is also ceremonial, as it is offered during *tequio* (a form of collective and voluntary work that is traditionally carried out in some Oaxacan towns).

Since it is a very energizing drink packed with vitamins, people would habitually drink it prior to a long day of work under the sun. The preparation of *coyol pozol* begins with nixtamalization.

Petra Valencia

"We use the smaller variety of heirloom corn that we have here, which we grow without fertilizers," says Mrs. Petra. Getting the almond or the "little coconut" from the *coyol* fruit is complicated. First, you have to peel the thick, brown or yellowish green rind. Then, you either bite or use your hands to remove the sticky pulp from each one —a labor intensive process. After that, with a stone or a heavy tool, you break open the *coyol*. Once the almond is retrieved, you can proceed to roasting. Juan José Valencia, Mrs. Petra's son, gets the fire going, cleans the clay *comal* (griddle) with a brush to remove any dirt or dust, and toasts each almond until their color changes to a dark brown, careful not to burn them as that would change the flavor. Once the almonds are evenly roasted, they are mixed with the nixtamalized corn and ground using either a *metate* or a hand mill. Juan grinds as Mrs. Petra slowly places the corn and *coyol* mix in the mill. The resulting dough is placed inside an *apaxtle* or large casserole. Water is poured over it as it is hand-mixed to achieve a moderately thick consistency. Sometimes, instead of water, pineapple *tepache* made with black pepper, cloves, and brown sugar is used. The *tepache* should be left to rest for five days for proper fermentation. After this process, the drink is served in *jícaras* (drinking gourds) or clay bowls. Sugar may be added as desired, but it is delicious as is because of the *coquito's* natural sweetness.

"There are a great many beverages that represent us Oaxaqueños, each region with their own ingredients that preserve our culture and give us a sense of identity," says Juan. Given that San Sebastián Coatlán's *pozol* is a ceremonial drink, it is difficult to find. However, on January 20th, during San Sebastián's festival, it is prepared in the village. It can also be found with Mrs. Petra Valencia, who says that, "If someone came and said to me, 'hey, I heard you make this drink,' I would get the ingredients so they could try it and learn how to make it, to keep the tradition alive because it is a beautiful thing."

Jesús González Rosas

09

Aguardiente

In the Middle Ages, Arabs sought the "elixir of life" that would keep the body eternally young. For this purpose, they developed the alembic, or still, to produce drinks with high alcoholic content. The beverages caused a burning sensation when drink, leading to the name *"aguas ardientes"* or "fire waters." This beverage tradition travelled to Spain with the Arabs and the Spaniards subsequently brought it to Mexico. This is how the drink, an important part of the culinary culture of Mexico, particularly of Oaxaca, came to exist. Mr. Jesús González Rosas, better known as Don Chucho, has dedicated his life to the production of *aguardiente* in El Sesteadero, a town belonging to the Putla municipality. "Since I didn't finish my studies this became my job. My dad had kept his still and after his death I was the only one interested in continuing the tradition," says Don Chucho. "Thanks to the *aguardiente* production, my husband's hard work has given me and my five children a better life," adds his wife, Hilda Figueroa García, who prepares *compuestos* with that same *aguardiente*. The main ingredient used for making *aguardiente* is sugar cane, a plant that is still heavily produced in Mexico. The very first *aguardiente* to reach Mexico was rum, arriving from the Caribbean. It quickly spread throughout the country under the name of *aguardiente*.

First he makes a *tepache* by fermenting wheat bran in wooden tubs with a little bit of water, sugar cane, or *piloncillo* (raw sugar). The sweeteners are gradually added to "strengthen the distillation." Slowly, the mixture will appear to be boiling because of the bubbles resulting from the fermentation. This process takes between seventy and eighty hours. For this, eight wooden tubs are used, six of 80 liters each and two of 160 liters.

Once it's been fermented, this *tepache* is transferred to the still using hoses. Through heat and fire, vapors or steam, referred to as "strength," are obtained. For this purpose, Jesús González Figueroa, Don Chucho's son, cuts some wood everyday. Once the steam reaches the top of the still, it turns into liquid and so the first drops of *aguardiente* (high proof liquor) sprout. On average, distillation time to fill a 190-liter container is about eight hours.

"When the *aguardiente* first drops it has a high alcoholic level of 75 proof, it is smooth and sweet. Then, after 150 liters have been distilled, the alcohol content starts going down," says Jesús. Looking back on history, it can be said that beer and other alcoholic beverages lowered *aguardiente* consumption in the region. Before, government officials would show up to collect taxes from *aguardiente* producers or to burn the distillation tools if these had not been paid. It is all regulated today and the beverage has once again become important. Twenty-five minutes from Putla Villa de Guerrero, taking the road towards Pinotepa Nacional, is El Sesteadero. There, *aguardiente* is sold in bulk and it is a delicacy that should not be missed.

Leova Martínez López y
Elia Martínez Martínez

10

Laxe Mecu
(atole meco)

San Matías Petacaltepec is a town within the San Carlos Yautepec municipality that is surrounded by agave fields mainly of the variety called *"chato"* (flat), which come from the Chontal region of Oaxaca. Similar to other indigenous communities, the elements that make up their worldview or cosmogony are deep and diverse. Among them is the *Laxe Mecu* or *Lashe Mecu* (*atole meco*), linked to Chontal authority figures. This drink is made with tender white corn, *mamey* fruit pit, or *pixtle*, and *panela* (raw sugar). This *atole* can be served cold or hot and it is also associated with men who work the land. The name *meco* comes from the unique color the drink gets from the corn and *panela*.

Leova Martínez López and Elia Martínez Martínez started making this *atole*, whose elaboration is solely assigned to women. "You grab the corn and take the husk off, then you remove all the kernels. Once the cob has been cleaned, you place it into a pot and fill it with water to boil," explains Leova Martínez, a San Matías Petacaltepec native. After the corn has been boiled, it is cooled down with a bath of cold water and then ground in a *metate*; the resulting *masa* (corn dough) is strained through a cheesecloth to remove any fibers or larger pieces. The filtered liquid is then boiled in a clay pot to cook the *atole* and left to cool down for the night. The leftover corn is briefly boiled in a little bit of water.

Elia uses a cane reed to release a few drops of the cooled *atole* into a *jícara* (dirnking gourd) filled with water. If the drops solidify as if they were pearls, the *atole* is ready. The following day, Leova places the *mamey* fruit pits directly over the fire to burn them. She then removes them from the fire and grinds them in a *metate* along with some *panela* and a little water to get a thick, dark liquid. Then she adds some of the *atole masa* (corn dough) from the previous day and mixes them together. "Many of the town's girls learn to make *atole* at the age of fifteen. This is an *atole* for authority figures. Every year, on January 6th, we prepare large quantities for everyone in town. When new authority figures take their positions, everyone goes to watch. Around 20 people prepare two large bags of corn together," says Luis Ángel Leodegario, who asked the authorities for permission so Elia and Leova could make the *Lashe Mecu* on this occasion. When this *atole* is made specifically for ritual purposes in San Matías Petacaltepec, six to eight tubs of it are made for about eight hundred people.

Likewise, when a guest coming from outside of town or a family member returns to the community, they are always welcomed with *atole meco* and *tamales*. This beverage is also made for weddings. "When there's a wedding it is important, when you are the father of the bride, for them to bring over some *atole* as a gift for your daughter, for having raised her," says Elia. A procession takes place following Christmas Eve and Christmas Day where women and men offer corn, beans, *copal* (a resin used as incense), and money, among other things, in gratitude for the good harvests and a celebration is held. A month later, on January 24th, baby Jesus is picked-up from the nativity scene and the Chontales, headed by two *mayordomos* (godfather figures for a celebration), offer *tamales* and *atole meco*. Just as in a church you would have bread and wine, in the *mayordomía* house there are *tamales* and *atole*. Elia serves the *atole* in a *jícara* (drinking gourd) while Leova adds the sweetener —a mix of *mamey* fruit pit and *panela*. This satisfying and thick drink can easily be enjoyed as a dessert.

11

Agua de
tlaciahual con panela

San Miguel Villa Sola de Vega is located a little over two hours away from Oaxaca City, within the state's Central Valleys. It sits on a mountain range where agave plants and sugar cane abound. It is a region for *palenques* (artisanal agave distilleries) and sugar mills, of *mezcal* and *panela* (raw sugar). The multi-crop *milpa* (a Mesoamerican cultivation system) is closely linked to corn. Nowhere in the world, apart from ancient Mexico, could a crop-growing system so deeply based on knowledge of plant, land, and community wisdom be found. Corn gave way to a complex pre-Hispanic worldview that, in turn, instructed the population on preparation techniques that made its enjoyment possible. In some parts of Oaxaca, the simplest corn cooking technique is called *tlaciahual*.

Gladys Hortensia Calvo García

Thus, the *milpa* is at once part of the San Miguel Villa Sola de Vega landscape. There, it is common to make *tlaciahual*, itself a product of the guelaguetza, a celebration that stands for coming together to help or "give each other a hand." "The men would go to do housework, whether it was sowing, weeding, or cleaning the corn, they would come together to help each other out, so the women would prepare this water," tells Gladys Hortensia Calvo García, a native of the town, who learned to prepare the drink at the age of ten.

To prepare the drink, the first step is to select the corn. It must be hard and have large white kernels free of dents. Gladys cuts all the kernels, cleans, and washes the cobs for the *tlaciahual*.

"You have to wait until it boils then you have to let it rest for a day so it completely cools down. Once cold, it is ground in a *metate* a couple of times until it is very fine," she explains. Gladys adds a bit of water and mixes it together by hand, removing all *chincaxtle* (fibers and larger pieces of corn), and later passes the mixture through a cheesecloth to remove all residue. She sweetens the filtered liquid with *panela* and adds an heirloom lime peel for flavor and aroma. *Tlaciahual* water is a beverage meant for everyday consumption as well as community gatherings or town parties. This drink is not sold or found on the streets. Gladys is a traditional cook who's highly sought-after for town celebrations, wakes, novenarios (a praying practice lasting for nine successive days), and even private parties. She specializes in traditional regional food and her wish is to promote Oaxacan cuisine, "transmitting to the younger generations what cooking means; reigniting the love for traditional foods because younger people no longer want to eat things like beans or home cooking, they prefer other dishes," she mentions while drinking some refreshing *tlaciahual* water in her restaurant, San Miguel.

12

Agua de
maíz
tostado

Melquiades Flores Pérez

San Matías Petacaltepec, a chontal indigenous community of Oaxaca, is a place that's closely linked to its oldest memories. There, people drink roasted corn flavored water at home.

Approximately eight thousand years ago, the people of Mesoamerica domesticated the native teocintle plant —a wild, ancient corn— creating a new plant. The corn's timeline coincided with that of fire, and women learned how to cook with it in ways their communities enjoyed, which lead to several cooking techniques, dishes, and beverages over time, including this roasted corn water.

Melquiades Flores Pérez, from San Matías Petacaltepec, learned hot to make roasted corn water with ground kernels thanks to her mother's and grandmother's teachings. This recipe has already been in use for three generations. Once all the kernels have been cut from the cob, the white grains are roasted on a *comal* until they almost burst. "You stir them so they don't scorch for about an hour, approximately, stir them along with the corncob until they change to a color that's between brown and black. Then it is ground dry to turn it into a powder. Once finely ground you add the *panela* (raw sugar)," explains Melquiades.

The ground powder is placed inside a *jícara* (drinking gourd) with a little bit of water and whisked. The beverage is generally enjoyed at lunchtime. There are some who bring the powder to the fields so they can prepare it there. This is a home beverage, not for sale, but if you were to visit San Matías Petacaltepec, most homes —such as Melquiades'— have this corn powder to prepare it.

Josefa Martínez Velázquez

13

Atole de
rabo de
iguana

Cocolmeca is a plant also known as "iguana tail." It has a vine that makes any drink it is added to frothy and it is also used for salads, memelas, *moles*, empanadas, and traditional stews from the Sierra Sur, where an indigenous Triqui community uses it to prepare a special drink. This beverage from the town of Paraje Pérez is so versatile it can be made as a soup or a broth. First, the "iguana tail" is gathered, preferably when tender. It is very easy to make because you put some corn to boil for twenty minutes and it is ready to be ground in a *metate*," says Josefa Martínez Velázquez, who's been preparing this drink since she was very young. The corn is then nixtamalized and after a day it is ground in a *metate*. The resulting *masa* (corn dough) is strained over a clay pot and cooked through. Then, *chile* puya's are ground and the "iguana tail" is cut into small pieces. Once the corn starts to boil, the *chile* and cocolomeca mixture is added along with avocado leaves and salt. In Paraje Pérez, the cocolmeca plant is found year round, so this drink is commonly enjoyed at people's homes during the morning, afternoon, or evening.

14

Tepache
de maíz

This drink can probably be traced back to pre-Hispanic times. Within the name lies the key ingredient that gave rise to the drink, since the word *tepiatl* —from which *tepache* derives— comes from the Nahuatl *tepitl*, "tender corn", and *atl*, "water." That is, "water from tender corn." Thus, *tepache* should technically always be made with corn, but the drink has evolved and today there are several varieties such as the famous pineapple *tepache*. However, in Tapanco, Zacatepec, an indigenous Tacuate community within the Sierra Sur, a roasted corn *tepache*

that's true to its etymology still exists today. Carmela Martínez Silva, a Tapanco native, started making this drink about thirty years ago with the help of a friend. At the *milpa*, she collects and selects the corn ears.

"These are left to dry out in the fields, then kernels are cut from the cobs, brought back to the house to be roasted until they turn a golden yellow, but not black and white because that means the corn is scorched," Carmela explains.

Carmela Martínez Silva

Carmela roasts the corn, washes and places it inside a clay pot with some brown sugar and water. "Tightly closed for two months." It is kept in an air-tight container to avoid contamination of the product.

"The *panela* (raw sugar) has to be a little white, here we call it 'coloradita', which is neither white nor black, because if the *panela* is very black then the *tepache* will come out too black," says Carmela. After two months, she opens the clay pot, stirs the liquid and strains it before pouring it into another pot, removing all sediments from it.

It is served in a *jícara* (drinking gourd) with ice, which refreshes the drink and balances the *panela's* intense sweetness.

This *tepache* is traditional during Carnival. "This drink is exclusively for Carnival and when there are local dances people will always ask for it; it is a town drink that's been in existence for many years," says Carmela.

One of her children already knows how to make this *tepache*. "My son, whose job is to sell the drink, will take my place after I'm gone," says Carmela, who's the only person that prepares and sells this *tepache* in town.

66

15
Chileatole con frijol nuevo

Chileatole has many variations. This version adds fresh beans to the beverage. "We go to the *milpa* to get the corn, which we call camagua when it's at the point right before becoming a cob, half-way between firm and tender. There, at the *milpa*, we cut the green beans, also at camagua point, which are a new addition since this *chileatole* comes served with beans. Camagua is when they are about to become beans, dried beans. Camagua is a Tacuate word that means halfway between ripe and firm. As we say, ripe is already old," explains Elizabeth Mateo Aparicio, also a native of El Tapanco, Zacatepec, who learned from her grandparents how to prepare the drink at the age of ten. It is a drink steeped in the indigenous home's worldview, of a tradition inherited from ancient times, of the marriage between corn and beans at their exact time of growth of

reproduction: camagua. After harvesting the corn, Elizabeth cuts the kernels off and grinds them using a *metate*. Once ground, she places the *masa* (corn dough) in a bowl filled with water and strains it through a cloth.

"We regularly use the cloth from the flour [sack] that's used to make bread and, once it is all ready, we place it in a clay pot filled with water over the stove to boil," says Elizabeth. After the corn' been boiled, it is rinsed with the leftover water from the strained *masa* (corn dough) and left to rest for half an hour. It will slowly start thickening and, during this time, Elizabeth also starts grinding heirloom costeño *chiles*. "Everything we use for the drink is grown here in the region," she says.

Elizabeth Mateo Aparicio

She adds some *epazote* leaves and the *chile*. She stirs the mix with a wooden spoon until it starts to boil, then adds some *panela* (raw sugar) and leaves it over the fire for two more hours. It must be cooked thoroughly so those who drink it don't become ill. "You also cook the beans on a different pot. Since they are new beans they have to be cooked, but they should not burst open; cooked through, but not to a breaking point, because the whole beans go into the *atole*. The beans are boiled only with salt," she says. Once the *atole* and beans are cooked,

Elizabeth serves the *chileatole* in a *jícara* (drinking gourd), strains the beans, and then adds them to the drink. During corn harvest —between March, July, and August— people enjoy the drink at home. "My grandfather used to tell me that this drink was only made here, because us Tacuates enjoy it this particular way as this is how they were taught to make it as well, and that it is something very special since you only had the privilege of drinking it during these dates," Elizabeth explains.

The *chileatole* with new beans is a delicate drink as carelessness can lead to it "getting cut." "Our belief is that if a person is preparing *chileatole* and a pregnant woman walks in, the drink will also be cut because she might crave it, something we refer to as 'eyeing it,' which is why the *atole* gets cut," she says.

"That's why our grandparents said that if we wanted to make *atole* we had to be patient, otherwise you'll end up wasting the cob."

Atole, says Elizabeth, should not be made while angry, as our feelings manifest in the drink's taste. You must be patient and always make it while in a good mood. "My town, El Tapanco, is one hundred percent indigenous Tacuate."

We still consume traditional foods and drinks. We also still do backstrap loom weaving, Tacuate clothing such as cotón, coyuchi *huipils*, our everyday clothing, and those made with linen and ribbons," concludes Elizabeth.

16

Agua de pixtle

María Santiago Cruz

In Santa María Zacatepec, Putla, the large majority of the population is Tacuate, one of the 16 indigenous groups from the state of Oaxaca. María Santiago Cruz learned to prepare *pixtle* (*mamey* fruit pit) water from her mother, who passed down this knowledge, at the age of fifteen. Before preparing it for the purpose of this book, many years had passed since she had last made it, but she still preserves in her mind and hands this inherited knowledge that's been passed down for many generations. In Tacuate (a language deriving from Mixtec), Mrs. María Santiago shared the following, "Usually, men are in charge of harvesting the corn, they are devoted to its cultivation so there's always corn, and they would ground it and make *nixtamal*. There would always be sowing, picking, and later cutting the kernels to make the *nixtamal*. From there you would make the *masa* (corn dough) in the *metate*. The most challenging thing is getting the *mamey* pit since it is seasonal," says Mrs. María through her grandson, Pedro López Merino, who served as our Spanish translator. *Mamey* is one of the tastiest fruits found in Mexico. It was formerly named *tesonzapote*, *tetzontzapotl* in Náhuatl, from *tetzontli* "*tesoncle*" (a porous rock), and *tzapotl* "*zapote*". That is, "*zapote tesoncle*," referring to the skin of the fruit, which has the color and roughness of the *tesoncle* or *tezontle*.

Today, it is called *mamey*, which the conquerors brought to Mexico from the Antilles. Its pit, or *pixtle* —from the Náhuatl *"pitzli,"* meaning "bone or seed"— is used to make many stews and drinks in Oaxaca. *Mamey* season is around March. It is picked from the tree on the second Friday of Lent and left to ripen. You can enjoy the fruit's flesh as well as making use of its sun-dried pit. Throughout *mamey* season, the pits are kept until the necessary amount is collected and then it's possible to use them for drinks such as *atole* or *pixtle* water. The pixtle or dehydrated pit is boiled for four whole days, never neglecting or putting out the fire. "If all the water evaporates you have to add more. And after four days, once the pits have cracked open and are no longer red on the inside, they are ready," explains María.

"Once they are thoroughly boiled, they are left outside in the sun for four days so the *mamey* pits lose all the leftover fat they have inside, until they are stiff and take a color similar to that of coal. It's a long process," adds María. Returning to the *nixtamal*, it is ground and a traditional white *atole* is prepared with it —the foundation of this drink.

The dried *pixtle* is ground and incorporation into the drink along with *panela* (raw sugar). The consistency is thick. In recent years, *atole* de *pixtle* consumption has greatly degreased in Zacatepec. "Previously, it was a common drink during Carnival, which happened during *mamey* season, and the authorities and masked dancers would drink it along with *tepache*," says Pedro. During Carnival, town's people would gather *mamey* for personal enjoyment and keep the pits in small sacks, but *mamey* is scarce today and, consequently, so is the *pixtle* to make *atole*. "They sell them now, so it's more of an economic issue. You can no longer walk around and pick some from a tree, now the owners complain and it is not allowed anymore," adds Pedro. Before, during Carnival, only the community authorities and a few select people would enjoy this drink, as it was so labor intensive. It was offered to them as an appreciation gift.

Mrs. María mixes the white *atole* base with the *pixtle* and *panela* syrup inside of a *jícara* (drinking gourd). The drink has a bit of white foam on top, similar to *tejate* from the Central Valleys of Oaxaca, due to the *pixtle's* fattiness.

17

Atole de

maíz tostado con granillo

Antonia Martínez Moreno

Toasting in a *comal* adds a delicious flavor to food. Some kernels, like that of "palomero" (popcorn) corn, will burst if over roasted, so it's vital to know what their exact cooking point is. "The kernels are taken off the cob with the hands, then placed over a *comal* to cook. Once done, the little kernels with pop. I really like drinking this *atole* because it's so tasty," says Antonia Martínez Moreno, a native of San Matías Petacaltepec, a town belonging to the indigenous Chontal community, who, at a very young age, learned how to prepare this drink from her mother. The corn is harvested dry, then cleaned, washed, and briefly roasted in the *comal*.

When the kernels start popping, Antonia removes them from the heat and places them inside of a bowl with water and soaks them for half an hour to soften, which will make the grinding process easier.

As Antonia grinds the corn, she removes the *chincaxtle* (fibers and larger pieces) along with the flesh from the kernels —the heart of the corn— and places it inside of a clay pot with boiling water. After an hour, she adds a little bit of *panela* (raw sugar) and stirs continuously to avoid the *atole* from burning or sticking. Once cooked, the drink is taken off the heat, served in a *jícara* (drinking gourd) and allowed to cool down.

What's exceptional about this drink is the texture the kernels add as well as the consistency of the *atole* as a whole. The roasted corn *atole* with kernels is meant for everyday family life, and not a celebratory or ritual drink. And, fortunately, community enjoyment of it keeps it current, especially thanks to the hands of women like Mrs. Antonia, who's transmitting this knowledge to her family and other women.

18

Café Labrador

Coffee arrived in Mexico at the end of the 18th century. Initially, it wasn't very successful as chocolate and *atole* were the drinks of choice. It reached Oaxaca in the 19th century, but the state's culinary richness prevented the black African concoction from popularizing. Yet, the coffee industry is going through an unusual boom because of the value given to the intimate link between land, climate, and the great care that is given to the coffee in order to obtain beans of the highest quality. This way, the farms are where a delicious cup of coffee is born.

Diracsema José José & Humberto Castro Reyes

Café Labrador is well aware of this, and that' why it is a brand offering a special green or roasted coffee at their own cafeteria in downtown Putla Villa de Guerrero, where you can taste their beans and those of 20 local growers who bring their delightful coffee and add to the effort of having a place where the culture of this aromatic drink is celebrated. In Putla's district, coffee beans are sown in the shade of other trees. It is an ecosystem that contributes to a harmonious environment for birds, reptiles, insects, and all the fauna and flora that simultaneously keep the coffee trees healthy. This has led to the formation of a remarkable coffee region. "I was born inside the coffee zone, the cradle of coffee, as we say in the mountains. My town is between one thousand and one nineteen hundred meters above sea level, which is where the following coffee plants grow: *Typica*, *Bourbón*, and *Mondo Novo*. We plant and do all the work ourselves and, the truth is, we do it with a lot of passion and love because we like doing it. We do everything, from sowing the coffee plant until we turn it into a cup of coffee," says Diracsema José José, who's originally from Zaragoza, Santa Cruz Itundujia, a community within the Putla municipality. The coffee selection is done by sampling each producer's product. If their quality standards are optimal, they start a business relationship with them to avoid using intermediaries. All their techniques, starting at the farm, must be carried out carefully. "We also want to teach the difference between a badly executed coffee process and a selection process where everything is well cared for starting the plant. How do the flavors and notes change?" says Diracsema. Coffee trees, like any other plant, have to ripen until they are at their prime, in order to start producing purified beans. In Putla, crops at an altitude of 700 meters are harvested from November to December. The higher it gets, the more harvesting season extends and it can go until April. Café Labrador is considered a specialty brand, as is selection starts at the farm. The collected beans are placed in an industrial coffee processing and grinding machine where they get divided by weight, size, color, and density. "We base our process on guidelines set by the SCA, the Specialty Coffee Association, and we go by their rules for selecting, roasting, toasting and what the industrial coffee machine has already selected," says Diracsema.

Once the beans have been separated, they are dried and later roasted. Roasting coffee is an art, only a master roaster knows how to neatly extract the best qualities from a coffee bean, for which he must know the bean variety, climate, altitude, and the method that will be used to make a cup with it, among other things. "The equipment is also important, if it responds well to temperature changes and air temperature adjustments. That's where knowledge comes in, the roaster's experience, knowing how to ensure these parameters so the coffee preserves its quality; otherwise, quality deteriorates. For example, a coffee rated at 86/90 can drop to an 80 rating if incorrectly roasted, so you have to be experienced enough to properly roast the beans," shares Humberto Castro Reyes, who's originally from San Juan Joluxtla, Cosoltepec, Huajuapan de León, and in charge of roasting at Café Labrador.

Humberto became a part of the coffee world by working at "dry-process," the place where "green" or "parchment" beans are selected for their qualities. Also at this place, sacks get filled and sealed, as well as sample analysis of different coffee varieties. "From there, we had the opportunity to work the bar, where we learned about espresso-based drinks and their preparation, and we were also working with some friends who have a tasting room, where we did coffee tastings, evaluating coffees from all regions of Oaxaca," shares Humberto. "Not all coffee tastes the same, we have to change that consumer culture, get people involved. I think Labrador belongs to the people, and I think I like that term because, who are the people involved? It's the producers and without them none of it could exist, and if there's no coffee, there's also no coffee bar," says Diracsema. Café Labrador can be found in Putla, right in front of the kiosk, as well as in Oaxaca City at Boulenc restaurant, located in the downtown area of the state capital.

There is not one type but a plethora of types of coffee drinks, from an americano to a cappuccino or a latte. Also, an americano can be enjoyed through various methods: French press, v60, Chemex, among others.

19

Cooperativa de

Mezcal Fanekantsini

Mezcal reveals a variety of flavors depending on the agave type, the *terroir*, the weather, and the producer's touch. There are fourteen *mezcal* agaves, plus many other varieties found in a region that extends from the the US-Mexico border to Central America and the Caribbean. Traditionally, it's been the *maestros mezcaleros* (*mezcal* masters) who've dedicated themselves to making the drink for generations; however, the earth and the plant, as well as the weather and times change. Sósima Olivera Aguilar, from the *Mezcal* Fanekantsini Co-op, is a *maestra mezcalera* who breaks with certain paradigms, making a worthy version of this ancestral alcoholic beverage and changing the perception surrounding the iconic distilled Oaxacan liquor. Sósima is originally from San Miguel

Suchiltepec, a town within the Yautepec municipality in the Sierra Sur. "I am the fourth generation of children who grew up in the *palenque* (an artisanal agave distillery.) This wonderful world that I grew up in seemed so impressive in my heart and mind that, at some point, I decided to do it myself. But, well, for that you had to go through the whole learning process, you had to watch and be observant. My dad used to make *mezcal* there in the *palenque* and we basically lived there with him," recalls the *maestra mezcalera*.

Mezcal is an alcoholic beverage that has gained popularity and fame because there is culture behind each bottle.

Sósima Olivera Aguilar

Thus, each drop must be appreciated, thanking the land and the producer for the gift, while the salesman has the obligation to fairly divide the economic gains to all those who participated in the production. This is why the *Mezcal* Fanekantsini Co-op strives to promote small, non-commercial brands of *mezcal*. "We used to produce the beverage to make some extra money for the family during a few months of the year; we only worked in *mezcal* production for a few months, but not the whole year, and its cultural value was more important than its economic value. It was always to trade for things like coffee, cheeses, to pay for labor, it was there as a kind of liquid gold, it was exchangeable, it didn't have this economic value but it's value, I would say, was much more important, it played a very important role in the town and the region," says Sósima with great conviction. The Co-op, Fanekantsini, a Chontal indigenous word meaning "three hummingbirds," began with only women, who came together to support each another and make their way in the *mezcal* world, traditionally a work only men in *palenque's* used to do. Fanekantsini is currently made up of seven families from Sola de Vega and San Miguel Suchiltepec. "At

one point, I said, 'we are only going to have women' and, well, over the years we came to the conclusion that we should also team up with men, I learned, and I like this wonderful experience of being a family. We are a family. And when it's your turn to lead the mule, distill, or make *tortillas*, it doesn't matter if you're male or female. When it's your turn, you do it," says Sósima. Fanekantsini uses *tequio*, a communal work system, for *mezcal's* sake and focuses their work on the field, from reproduction of regional agaves, their natural growth, flowering and maturity, to sharing their knowledge of the distilled liquor with local producers, always working as a team. "This Co-operative space was created so more people had jobs. The one in Sola de Vega makes the most impact in that sense, because the idea started there, and people go there from other towns to make *mezcal*. For example, when a town is having a celebration they come and ask to use the *palenque*, they make their *mezcal* and that's it, they're not commercializing it or selling it, it's for their parties," says Sósima. *Mezcal* is an essential drink. *"Para todo mal, mezcal, y para todo bien también"* or, "when all is wrong, *mezcal*, when all is well as well," goes saying in Oaxaca.

And it is extremely true, as the distilled liquor is a part of everyday life, linked to Oaxacan identity from the day they are born to the day they die. In some communities, they give pregnant women —right before they give birth— a dose of *mezcal* diluted with *piloncillo* (raw sugar), which works as a sedative and energizer, helping the mother with childbirth.

"When we had a fever from a stomach or throat infection, my mother would bathe us in *mezcal* and wrap us in blankets, like a little taco, and then we would start to sweat, and she would come touch you and say, 'Okay, it's ready! Also for the nerves, for all those things that sometimes science can't explain, it was something magical, so much that you would be cured from one day to the next," continues Sósima.
San Miguel Suchiltepec is located just over two thousand meters above sea level, which is why they have such harsh winters. "My grandmother would wake up to make *tortillas*, she'd make herself a cup of coffee with about a quarter of *mezcal*, and continue making *tortillas*.

Then, I'd ask her: grandma, why are you sweating?' It was cold out and she was sweating, and she'd answer: it's cold, I had a bit of *mezcal*," recalls Sósima. All *mezcal* goes through the same elaboration process. The *pencas* (agave cores) are roasted and ground, then the mosto (the resulting liquid and fibers from the ground, roasted agaves) is fermented in tubs, and the juices are distilled. What makes them different is the people who carry out these processes, as it is them who add the touches that make each *mezcal* unique. That is why Sósima keeps a warehouse full of glass jars, where they can keep a record of the various *mezcals* they have produced.

The area has a very strong *mezcal* culture, which is why, in front of the town of San Lorenzo Jilotepequillo, there's a character named Fanekantsini, a pre-Hispanic figure set on a hill, that only authority figures visit every year. During their annual ceremony, food, cups, candles and *mezcal* are offered. The indigenous Chontal Co-operative working with women to bring a new perspective to the old beverage took their name from that symbol.

Valles Centrales

This is the geographical, political, and social heart of Oaxaca, as well as the state's best known region. Oaxacan people simply call it, "The Valleys." It borders four of the eight regions of the state. To the north with the Mixteca, the Cañada, and the Sierra Norte; to the south and west with the Sierra Sur; to the east with the Sierra Norte and Sierra Sur. The region is comprised of 121 municipalities belonging to seven districts: Etla, Zaachila, Zimatlán, Centro, Tlacolula, Ejutla, and Ocotlán.

This region, as its name implies, is an area where three river valleys converge: that of Etla, Tlacolula, and Zimatlán-Ocotlán, also called Valle Grande—all located between the Nudo Mixteco (Mixtec Knot), the Sierra Juárez, and the Sierra Madre del Sur. It extends to cover five percent of the total area of the state of Oaxaca. Although the Central Valleys aren't physically homogenous, the weather tends to be mild and pleasant. The Etla Valley is slightly more humid, which makes the land more fertile, allowing important cereal and fruit crops to grow.

Generally, the land has a bountiful supply of cornfields. In fact, it is possible that corn originated in the Central Valleys' highlands, which would explain the great genetic variety of the plant in Oaxaca, where 35 types are found —54% of all those found in Mexico. The Central Valley region is also famous for their handmade textiles, fabrics made from palm and cane reed, and pottery.

20

Agua de limón rallado

Although limes are Asian, the citrus industry arrived in Mexico during the sixteenth century along with the Spaniards, which explains why the use and enjoyment of the plant is so ingrained in our culinary culture. However, the first commercial Mexican lime plantations weren't established in Oaxaca until the twentieth century.

While so-called "Mexican limes" have not triumphed abroad because of their size, seeds, and sour flavor, the Mexican population loves them for those very reasons, impacting the region's culinary culture as its acidity strongly influences the characteristics of the country's food, something that runs even deeper in Oaxaca. The Central Valleys' *agua de limón rallado* (lime zest water) is quite different in terms of flavor, color, and taste from a lime water or a traditional limeade. At "*Aguas Casilda*," in the city of Oaxaca, this is undoubtedly one of the most popular drinks. "*Aguas Casilda*" opened in 1926, preparing various flavors of *aguas frescas*; the stand is a true staple of the state capital's Benito Juárez Market, which is why it is always packed with people who come for one of their multiple refreshing offerings.

Humberta Natividad Cruz

89

Irinea Valera Abella

21

Horchata
con tuna

This is one of the most popular drinks sold at *Aguas Casilda*, a stand in the Benito Juárez mark in the city of Oaxaca. There isn't a single type of *agua de horchata* in Mexico or the world, as there are many beverages sharing this name. A distinguishing feature all the variations of the drink have in common is their white color, but the ingredients and preparation techniques are numerous depending on their place of origin. The word *horchata* comes from the Latin *hordeata*, "made with barley," which perhaps comes from the Mozarabic *hordeum*, "barley." Romans were introduced to it in Egypt and, among Arabs, this beverage was made with ground and strained yellow nutsedge (a tuber) that was mixed with water and sugar. Romans brought the word to Spain and, from there, it came to Mexico, even though here *horchata* is traditionally made with rice, coconut, and barley, perhaps due to the Manila Galleon's influence.

The *horchata* at *Aguas Casilda* is made with rice and a touch of prickly pear, melon, and walnuts. This *agua fresca* recipe, "was taught to us by our aunt, our father's sister, María Teresa Valera Flores, and our grandmother. Everyone knew our aunt as Chata or Chatita. And mainly, we learned from my grandmother saying, 'Ok, give me the fruit, wash the knife, pay attention to how it's done,' learning as with all jobs, little by little. Washing dishes, bringing things, it's like at an office, you start at the bottom," shared Irinea Valera Abella and Berta Natividad Cruz, granddaughters of Casilda Flores Morales, founder of *Aguas Casilda*, a landmark of *aguas frescas* in Oaxaca. "Sometimes people ask us, 'how many kilos of rice, how many almonds, or how much cinnamon?' but we hardly ever weigh anything, we eyeball it, we know the measurements by heart," Irinea explains as she prepares the *aguas*.

Preparation for Casilda's *horchata* begins 24 hours in advance, since you have to cook the almonds and peel each one by hand. The rice is soaked in water overnight to be washed the following day. Once ready, it's brought to a mill along with the almonds and cinnamon to turn into a paste. During high season, the work begins at five in the morning and at seven during low season.

After returning from the mill, water is added to the paste to be strained through a special cheesecloth in order to extract all its flavors. This special cheesecloth employed to decant the concentrate can be reused for up to fifteen days, since daily use wears down the fabric, as the cloth's surface is scraped during the filtering process to remove all sediments. Once this *horchata* concentrate is obtained, it is brought to the market stand and placed inside a large clay pot. The addition of red prickly pears gives the Oaxacan version of the drink a unique touch. "Usually, people won't drink it if there's no prickly pear in it. It's not the kind of prickly pear that has large seeds as many foreigners believe, and it's also not hard. We don't even blend it as it's very soft," says Humberta while crushing the intensely red prickly pears.

During prickly pear season, *Aguas Casilda* offers that agua fresca flavor but, otherwise, the business only uses them for the *horchata*. "We get the prickly pears free of thorns. They come from nearby Ocotlán and once season there ends they are brought from the Tehuacán area," adds Humberta.

The *horchata* recipe began its journey from the business' early days: "October 15, 1926 is the date we celebrate the business' anniversary. My grandmother used to say that her mother also sold *aguas* as well as her aunt, who would sell at the *zócalo* (main plaza). My grandma started the the Casilda name —she was 16 when it all began," tells Irinea.

Irinea and Humberta say that, "You have to love your work so it prospers and then you make an effort to be up early. The reward you get is people saying how good the *aguas* are as well as keeping the name alive. Even though she is no longer with us her name lives on with all of those who say their *aguas* are from Casilda."

Horchata is served in a glass over a little bit of crushed prickly pear, pieces of melon, and some pecans, which adds to the presentation and flavor that pleases all those who try it. The *Aguas Casilda* stand in the Benito Juárez market is always colorfully decorated depending on the season and packed with people. Behind the bar, you can see more than ten jugs with different flavored *aguas* and, in the background, you can also see a wall with photographs and acknowledgments of the shop's long trajectory. It is a place that one shouldn't miss when visiting the city of Oaxaca.

22

Agua de

zapote negro

A *zapote* (sapote or sapodilla) is a delicious fruit. Its name comes from the Nahuatl *tzapotl*, which was the name used for "any sweet-tasting fruit" in the pre-Hispanic era. In Mexico, there's a huge variety of *zapotes,* among which is the "black zapote," named after the fruit's pulp color, used in Oaxaca to make a very tasty drink. The black *zapote* (a species of persimmon) is a fruit of size and shape similar to a tomato, but with a smooth green skin and an intensely dark black or brown flesh. Its flesh is abundant, of thick consistency and a velvety texture. A couple of interesting facts: apparently, this *zapote* helps counter the progress of vitiligo and it is also said to improve blood quality. This is a very sweet-tasting fruit that feels quite unctuous on the palate. When it ripens, its green skin darkens and becomes fragile to the touch —this is the ideal time to enjoy it.

Humberta Natividad Cruz & Irinea Valera Abella

"To make *agua de zapote*, youy have to wait until the *zapote* is ready. My grandmother taught us that it had to be ripe like this one," says Irinea from *Aguas Casilda* while holding out a ripe and soft black sapote. The *aguas* stand that Mrs. Casilda's granddaughter manages today sometimes gets the black *zapote* from San Andrés Huayapam, a neighboring town of Oaxaca City. Sometimes it's brought from Cuicatlán, a town in the Cañada region that also has an abundance of black *zapote*. If they arrive green and unripe, they are placed inside a basket with some newspaper to gradually ripen and, once ready, they are used to make the sophisticated drink.

Once the *zapotes* have been selected, Irinea and her sister, Humberta, wash and disinfect them to be processed whole, skin included. "We use a strainer for that process. There, we remove what we call the crown of the *zapote*, the stem, we remove it and we start beating it," says Irinea, who has more than eighteen years of experience in the elaboration of *aguas frescas*. Once the black *zapote* has been mashed, Irinea strains it to remove the skin and seeds. The consistency is very thick. Then, water is added to the pulp so the *zapote* is, "neither water nor thick," she explains. Once the water has been strained, freshly squeezed orange juice is added to the drink along with chopped pecans and a little sherry, which is a spectacular touch.

The fruit's season begins in September and it is the best time to enjoy this Oaxacan delight

23

Agua de chilacayota

The *chilacayota* is a type of squash, or pumpkin, similar to a watermelon. Its name comes from the Nahuatl *tzilacayotli*, from *tzilac* "smooth," and *ayotli,* "pumpkin," meaning "smooth pumpkin," as it doesn't have the longitudinal grooves of other pumpkins that give their skin the appearance of having ribs. Although there are some who say the name comes from *tzilictic,* "something with a clear sound," and *ayotli*, "pumpkin," meaning "pumpkin that sounds well," as its thick skin makes a beautiful, vibrating sound when tapped, different from other fruits of the same family.

It is a gourd that's endemic to Mexico. When unripe, its flesh is soft, its shape slightly oval, and its skin light green with white spots, similar to an heirloom squash. In many states where it's grown, it is used as a vegetable to prepare several stews. When ripe, it can measure between twenty to twenty-five centimeters. On the outside, it holds to its smooth texture of various green shades and yellowish-white spots. Inside, its seeds are usually black and its flesh is juicy, white, and so fibrous that it looks like tangled hair after cooking that can also be used to make a dessert called "angel hair."

In Oaxaca, *agua de chilacayota* is commonly made in several regions of the state, but one of the tastiest is the one made at *Aguas Casilda*.

Humberta Natividad Cruz

"Sometimes they come sell freshly picked *chilacayotas*. Those still have a green stem and there are some with such hard skin that it takes a lot of work to cut them open as the knife bounces back," says Humberta Natividad Cruz, granddaughter of the legendary Mrs. Casilda, who keeps her grandmother's tradition alive. "Usually, we use about three *chilacayotas* a day. During Samaritana (a Oaxacan celebration where *aguas frescas* are gifted to all who ask for it) we use about forty or fifty, it is on the fourth Friday of Lent, and during low season we use two *chilacayotas* to make the water," says Irinea Valera Abella, also a granddaughter of Mrs. Casilda. The work to prepare the beverage starts at seven in the morning. The first step is cutting the *chilacayota*, "You have to know how to cut it properly so the "worm" can be removed, which is a little stubble that my grandmother said is bitter," says Humberta while cutting the *chilacayota* with a lot of effort since the skin is hard. Then, she removes and discards the stubble.

The *chilacayota* is cut into six pieces that are places in water, separating the seeds that are to be washed independently. During this process, the water slowly fills with foams, as if soap had been added. This is due to the saponin, a natural component of the fruit.

Afterwards, the pieces are placed inside a large pot, along with the seeds, and cooked until soft. You have to wait for them to boil, checking their consistency with a spoon or knife, until they feel soft, which means the *chilacayota* is ready. "We don't have a time for how long it takes, know when it's ready," says Humberta. Once the *chilacayota* is cooked through it is carefully drained and ice is then added to the pot to cool down in order to scrape the pulp with a knife. At once, *panela* (raw sugar) is boiled and all impurities such as the foam, pieces of cane, or even bees are removed. Also, limes previously soaked in water are peeled, cinnamon sticks are sliced, and these are added to the *agua de chilacayota*.

"At the market stand, when we stir it using a *jícara* (drinking gourd), the lime peel starts releasing its flavor," adds Irinea.

At the market, they occasionally add sweetener if the costumer wants. It is also possible to add some pecans, and *chilacayota* water can even be mixed with pineapple or lime zest water —two combinations that locals frequently request. *Chilacayota* season is in September, but this unique beverage that requires one to use a spoon to eat the pulp, as with a dessert, can be enjoyed all year round. This is one of the most popular *aguas* at *Aguas Casilda*.

Lucrecia Ruiz Ruiz

24 Tejate

Tejate is a pre-Hispanic drink closely linked to the first indigenous Zapotecs of the Central Valleys of Oaxaca. Traditionally, it is made with two types of cocoa (red and white), nixtamalized corn, *pixtle*, "rosita de cacao (little rose of cocoa)" and sugar. Apparently, the name comes from *texatl*, from the Nahuatl *textli*, "flour," and *atl*, "water." Meaning, "mealy water." Zapotecs refer to the *tejate* as *cu'uhb* and to the foam as *ghilo cu'uhb*, meaning "*tejate* flower."

Lucrecia Ruíz makes *tejate* in San Andrés Huayapam, a town about twenty minutes from Oaxaca City. For the past 48 years, she's been repeating the same process to make this fine drink. One of the ingredients is the "*rosita de cacao* (little rose of cocoa)," the flower of a tree that is emblematic in the town. "We have *rosita de cacao* here in Huayapam. The tree needs enough water and a lot of attention to bloom all year long," which also guarantees *tejate* for the whole community. First, corn is nixtamalized, then the rest of the ingredients are roasted over low heat in the *comal* griddle, moving them around with a brush so they toast evenly. Later, the corn is ground and the remaining ingredients are incorporated.

The resulting paste is placed in a very deep and wide green clay pot, and water is added while they mix with one hand for an hour until it foams. When that *tejate* "flower" or foam covers the top of the pot, it's ready.

Tejate is served in a *jícara* (drinking gourd) and, since it is a round container, using a reed ring as a supporting base is necessary. It is also served with a wooden stick to more easily enjoy the foam. Making *tejate* is a labor and time intensive work. The *tejateras* (*tejate* makers) endanger their sight and lungs to the smoke from roasting the ingredients and, for the grinding process, they must kneel over the *metate* for four hours. Mixing the drink also takes a great deal of effort, as it takes an hour by hand.

This dedication to make good quality and delicious *tejate* should be appreciated, considering the *tejateras'* effort to preserve our heritage and culinary traditions. Apart from being tasty, *tejate* is a good source of calcium, iron, fiber, protein, carbohydrates, and healing properties for stomach ailments.

You can sample a delicious *tejate* in the streets of Oaxaca, but in the Benito Juárez market, at the La Flor de Huayapam store, you can enjoy this delight with Lucrecia Ruíz, who makes it all year long. Meanwhile, in San Andrés Huayapam, it can be found on weekends as well as every Palm Sunday, when they celebrate *Tejate* Festival to honor one of the most important beverages of Oaxaca.

René Sánchez Ramírez

25

Tepache de frutas

La Ciénega, a town within the Zimatlán municipality, has a treasure in its fruit *tepache*. It is a *tepache* made with an earth oven, a technique that's unique for this traditional drink. The earth oven is a type of incandescent well that originated and developed in ancient Mexico before spreading throughout Mesoamerica and elsewhere in the continent. In Yucatán, the Mayans named it *pib*, and in central Mexico it is called "*barbacoa*" (barbecue), a Caribbean word that is used today for this type of oven that adds such unique flavor, smell, consistency, texture, and temperatures to all the food that is cooked in it.

To this earthen well, "you have to add a little fire, embers, because that's what starts the fermentation process; the decomposition of the fruit," explains Mr. Félix René Sánchez Ramírez, a La Ciénega native, who started making this drink along with his wife, María, over forty years ago. Mr. René works from January to March in the production of *panela* (raw sugar), which is when the mill behind his house operates. They do the entire process, from cutting the cane at the fields, to grinding it, boiling its juice, separating the product, and selling it. They make the *panela* at night, until dawn, so they can withstand the high temperatures from the ovens, and because it is when there are fewer bees surrounding the molasses being released from the sugar cane juice. At the Sánchez family backyard, there is a smoking kitchen and two earth ovens, one for making *barbacoa* and the other for making *tepache*, a drink that in Oaxaca is not necessarily made from pineapple, as the word is also used for low fermentation beverages made from agave *pulque* and fruits.

A fire is lit in the oven and Mr. René adds the *bagasse* (the remains of dry cane), which serves as firewood. Slowly the fire dissipates, leaving the red hot embers. A one-hundred-liter capacity clay pot is then placed inside the hot earth oven walls. "The important thing is that it's hot enough to start fermenting. The *panela*, *pulque*, and fruit are responsible for making a beautiful drink." While the pot is heating-up, the fruits are cut. Mr. René uses only heirloom fruits, as they add a unique flavor to the drink. Among other fruits he uses: apple, sugar cane, pineapple from the Sierra, and the peel of a *castilla* banana, though never the actual flesh of the banana as it thickens the drink. He also adds cinnamon, *panela*, water and *pulque*, which serves as the base for the drink. He thoroughly mixes the fruits using a cane reed, then covers the pot with bags to prevent it from overflowing. He makes a cross adorned with flowers and places it on top of the top to bless the drink and prevent it from going bad. With the pot covered, he then waits four to five days until it's at the perfect point of fermentation. "A day early it is very weak, but at the fifth day it is tastier, richer. The average is four days," says Mr. René.

Exactly four days later, he uncovers the pot. He removes the cross, the bags, and all the gratifying aromas of the fruits are strongly revealed as he opens the pot. Then he stirs the fruits sitting at the bottom of the pot with a cane reed and, with the help of his wife and nieces, he begins taking all the *tepache* out. The outcome is a refreshing drink that has a fruity taste with slightly bitter notes that result from the *pulque* and fermentation.

The *tepache* will continue fermenting. At day five, its flavor intensifies and people will add chili, chopped onion, and a few pinches of worm salt. That way, it transforms into a different drink. You can get two drinks out of a single pot, it all depends on when each is enjoyed, but both are delicious. "Usually, the beverage is prepared for a *mayordomía*, a wedding, a *quinceañera*, parties. A *mayordomía* in Oaxaca is when a family or person throws a party for a saint and invites all of their friends and town's people," Mr. René says to close. This delicacy can be sampled in La Ciénega, Zimatlán, with Mr. René and María, "those who make *panela* or *trapiche*."

26
Chocolateatole de
San Antonino
Castillo Velasco

Chocolate *atole* is a traditional drink from San Antonino Castillo Velasco that's made with cocoa and corn. And although in other towns there is also a drink with the same name, sometimes its ingredients or preparation are different.
"I started [making the drink] at the age of twelve, with my baptism godmother, Apolonia Alonso Sánchez, who was the one to teach me how to roast, peel, and grind," explains María Luisa López, a native of San Antonino Castillo Velasco, a town near Ocotlán de Morelos, which is 30 minutes away from the state capital.

María Luisa López

"If I couldn't do it, I would get a beating, because that's how it was before, with beatings, and since I didn't know how to read, she would tell me I had 'to work, daughter, since you don't know how to read,' but I could work," continues María Luisa as she separates the corn kernels with a threshing machine, confirming that children were taught that way in the past, with a beating for every mistake made while preparing something in the kitchen.

María Luisa grinds the kernels in a *metate* and then places the *masa* (corn dough) in a clay pot to be cooked. The corn will be ready in an hour. The chocolate is prepared separately.

To serve de chocolate *atole*, the *atole* is first poured in a *jícara* (drinking gourd), then the chocolate foam is added. The drink is served with an *alcahuete*, a wooden stick for stirring.

The sweet drink is served hot, though the foam is cold. You can sample the beverage everyday in San Antonino, specifically at the market, although I recommend trying Maria Luisa's, who also offers *pinole*, chocolate, and powder chocolate.

27

Chocolate atole con cacao blanco

Chocolate *atole* is a drink that is prepared in at least three different municipalities of the Central Valleys. Each one is prepared differently due to Oaxaca's diversity, where drinks can completely change from one town to another. The chocolate *atole* from Teotitlán del Valle is very different from the other beverages with the same name, as it is made with wheat, rice, and *pataxte* or white cocoa, a cocoa that is fermented underground for over six months, making it one of the drinks with the most sophisticated processing techniques. The *pataxte* is a type of cocoa used since pre-Hispanic times that is often confused with the fruit from the regular cocoa tree as they are very similar, which generates many mistakes and controversies. But traditional cooks can differentiate and identify each of them very well. "I learned [to cook] from my mother when I was ten-years-old, but I already knew how to make this specific drink by the time I was fifteen.

Carina Santiago

My mother is my teacher and has taught me, but so has my mother-in-law, and with her I finished my training by learning about other flavors. Each house has their own seasoning. I have two great teachers," says Carina Santiago, a native of Teotitlán del Valle who, besides cooking, does weaving on a loom, an artisanal craft that's very representative of the Zapotec people. The foundation of the chocolate *atole* is the white cocoa or *pataxte*, but this cocoa must be fermented beforehand. First, a pit inside the ground is dug, about one-meter-deep, where water is added little by little to achieve a precise, moist consistency in the pit, where the cocoa will be placed. Having done the above mentioned, it is covered with *petates* (woven palm bedrolls) and left to ferment for a period between six and nine months. Once it's been fermented, it is washed thoroughly, spread over mats and sun-dried. "On preparation day, the redest and most beautifully textured cocoa is chosen," explains Carina. The cocoa is washed, dried, and roasted on a clay griddle over low heat to toast evenly.

The same process is repeated with the cinnamon, corn, wheat, and rice. Once all the ingredients are ready, they are ground in a *metate* to obtain a dry paste, cinnamon mixture, a cocoa without a shell, wild rice, wheat, corn, and white cocoa, which is the mildest ingredient as well as the protagonist of this *tlaciahual* (boiled corn) drink.

Meanwhile, the *tlaciahual* is cooked for about twenty to twenty-five minutes. Then the corn is left to rest overnight so it cools and softens. The resulting liquid must be ready before the dry paste.

Then, a little cold water is poured in an *apaxtle* (a large clay pot) from Atzompa (a town in Oaxaca that's famous for their clay pottery), and the paste is slowly incorporated to it, which will dissolve as it is mixed in, creating the characteristic foam of the drink. "We must be meticulous with both our hygiene and that of the tools because it is a drink of the gods, it is a delicate drink, and if we're not meticulous enough and use a *metate* meant for *chiles*, or a container used for fat,

we won't achieve this foam, it can sour, it just won't work out," explains Carina while grinding the white cocoa.

To serve the drink, the cook grabs a clay container and first pours in the cooked *atole*, adding a touch of honey to sweeten it, and then tops it with the foam —somewhat bitter because of the cocoa— places an *alcahuete* (wooden stick for stirring and drinking) on it, and it's ready to be enjoyed!

This drink, which is very special in the Central Valleys, is served alongside a plate of delicious *"higaditos de fandango"* (a soupy egg and poultry dish) for breakfast. It is enjoyed during *mayordomías* or patron saint celebrations.

Catalina Chávez Lucas

28
Cerveza de piña

Generally, beer is a fermented mix of malt, water, yeast, and hops, to which you can add some other ingredients to give the drink a unique touch of flavor. However, in Oaxaca, there is a beverage with that name that bears little resemblance with the classic drink, as it has *pulque*, *panela*, pepper, cinnamon, roasted corn, and a bit of beer —with the pineapple being the most predominant flavor. Although, in Mexico, the first beers arrived to the Amecameca region in the 16th century, the drink was not successful as there already were many other tasty fermented beverages, such as *pulque* and *curados*, *tepache*, or *tesgüino*. It wasn't until the end of the 19th and 20th centuries that the brewing industry we know today grew in Mexico. "My mother prepared this drink, it was one of the first things she started making. I started as a kid just like this, watching her prepare it for Tlacolula's *mayordomías*, and they would come ask her to make just the pineapple beer. It's not as common anymore, but my mom continues to make it on special occasions for the family and we serve it as a drink here at the restaurant," says Catalina Chávez Lucas, a traditional cook from Tlacolula.

Preparations for the drink start a day in advance, when Catalina goes to the neighboring town of Matatlán to *pulque*. Upon her return, she roasts some corn in the *comal*. "Roasted corn has something that cannot fail as it is what helps the pineapple ferment," she explains while grinding the roasted corn.

Then, she washes and cuts the pineapple into small cubes and transfers it to the *metate* to be ground as well. She slowly incorporates some pepper and *panela*, obtaining a very thick liquid. She places the resulting paste into a clay bowl with some fresh water and, one by one, she adds the rest of the ingredients.

She will then let the drink rest and ferment overnight. The following day, she decants it, filtering it so it's ready to be served at a party or *mayordomía*. "This is of great significance in the Tlacolula valley. We call it the *tepache* 'uncapping.' When Jesus blessed the wedding of Cana [Canaan] and blesses the wine, during the May celebrations, then comes the *tepache* uncapping, and we dance after prayer," says Catalina.

Pineapple beer is a drink that is only made for *mayordomías* or town celebrations, although Catalina, serves it every Sunday at her restaurant, Mo-Kalli, as she wants people to be able to enjoy it.

Bernardino Salvador Arellanes Cruz

29
Ron

Sugarcane first arrived to the Americas from the Canary Islands in the 16th century. In the Caribbean, Spaniards booster its cultivation. There, it grew exponentially and black people —who had arrived to replace Taínos who had died from diseases introduced by the new inhabitants— made rum their drink. Then, once sugarcane spread through the continent, the drink traveled with it, gaining popularity. Mexico was no exception, and neither was Oaxaca.

As with the sugarcane, the alembic, or still, needed to be circulated to make rum and *aguardientes* that have become of extreme importance to the communities that produce them.

"I was curious about it since I got started when my grandfather planted the sugarcane. They were from La Ciénega, Zimatlán, and they arrived to this town in 1933, and they brought the sugarcane from there as it was used often for decorating Day of the Dead altars. I had the idea of making rum, I researched, went all around, went to the *trapiches* (sugarcane mills), around San Porvenir, around the Cañada, we were around there. At first I thought about making *aguardiente*, since rum is more delicately made, and we experimented until we got it right," says Bernardino Salvador Arellanes Cruz, who's originally from San Sebastián Etla.

Mr. Salvador bet on rum and bought thermometers, saccharimeters, breathalyzers, and all the tools needed to make a drink as good as the acclaimed brands. His rum is one hundred percent natural as he doesn't use artificial fertilizers or soil aggregates. His fertilizer is organic and the only ingredient he uses is the heirloom sugarcane he and his family grow.

"To start, the land must be well prepared, the plowing, you have to give it lots of sun and have no weeds, and then you make 1.60-meter-wide grooves, and then the sugarcane is chopped as the sugarcane itself is the seed. And after two years it's quite sweet and here we try for it to have a high Brix reading, we've gotten it as high as twenty degrees Brix," says Mr. Salvador.

After two years of the sugarcane being planted, it's sugary enough to make a good rum. Following the harvest, the sugarcane is sent to a *trapiche*, where the juices are extracted to be poured into a 750-liter tub. Using a pump, the liquid is transferred to a fermentation container. Depending on the weather, the process will take between eight to twelve days. The higher the temperature, the faster the fermentation.

Sugar content is measured using the saccharimeter, water separates from the alcohol and once the it reaches zero point, the liquid is transferred to the still that's been previously heated with firewood. Once boiling, the steam will move through the columns, the onion head, and the condenser coil. And there, as it moves through the water level, the steam turns to liquid because of condensation, then it precipitates into a collection cup where the "heads" are separated, meaning, the liquid with the highest alcoholic content. That's when the rum is ready.

"Now, if I want it aged, I transfer it into the barrels and after six months it becomes a *reposado* and after a year it becomes an *añejo*. We have some that have been aged for three and almost four years: *reposado*, *añejo*, and white," explains Mr. Salvador.

Currently, the Rey Eteco rum is in the process of registering for sale in commercial stores. However, their three varieties can be purchased at El Sazón de Etla restaurant, located in San Sebastián Etla, ten kilometers from Oaxaca City, or at their factory in the town of Eteco, which is open to the public.

30
Atole
de panela

Atole de *panela* is an everyday *atole*, a specialty from the town of Tlacolula de Matamoros. In the morning or at night, this beverage is ubiquitous and thoroughly enjoyed in this community. It is also prepared for parties, wakes, Catholic Holy Days, processions, prayers for the Lord of Tlacolula or for the Virgin of Asunción, and other patron saint celebrations. "This is a very common drink. We currently prepare it with yellow corn, but it can be prepared with any type of corn available at home," says Catalina Chávez Lucas, a traditional cook from Tlacolula de Matamoros. The first is knowing which corn will be used. There are several options available in the area. According to some specialists, the origins of corn are linked to the Central Valleys and, from there, it was domesticated elsewhere in the world. There are 64 varieties of corn in Mexico, many of them found in Oaxaca, giving different flavors, smells, colors, and textures to the beverages that incorporate them.

Catalina Chávez Lucas

Once the grain has been selected, the kernels are taken off the cob and turned to *tlaciahual* (boiled corn). Then it is ground, and the *masa* (corn dough) is rinsed with water, hand-washed, and the *chincaxtle* (fibers and corn skins) is removed. The water where the *masa* is sitting is then decanted into a large jícara (drinking gourd) and the remaining kernels are removed by hand.

A clay pot filled with the grainless water is placed over an *anafre* (coal burning stove) to boil. Slowly, fresh water is added along with *panela*. It must be continuously stirred as *atole* can easily stick to the pot. Using a wooden stick that she inherited from her grandmother, Catalina stirs the drink as it boils.

"If your *tlaciahual* is good everything will turn out fine, but if your corn is overcooked it will lose its sweetness," Catalina emphasizes.

Thanks to her mother, Catalina learned how to prepare this *atole* when she was seven years old. "My mother worked in the kitchen and when I came back from school I had to make the *tlaciahual* and after bringing it down I had to go where my mother was working.

Since we sold *atole* everyday, it was a daily duty. It is one of those things that make an impact on you, you know them by heart, for us it is a very simple drink because it is a part of yourself," she says.

Atole de panela is generally served in a clay bowl.

Catalina serves this delicious drink at her restaurant, Mo-Kalli, located in Donají street in the Tres Piedras neighborhood. It can also be found starting at seven in the morning at the local Tlacolula market. The drink is so popular that there are people in town who ride tricycles from house to house selling *atole de panela*.

31
Chocolate
de agua

Cacao (cocoa) is a word belonging to the Mixe-Zoquean family that the Olmecs of ancient Mexico have been using, as kakawa, since the year 1000 BC. Soconusco and Chontalpa were two production areas closely linked to high quality fruits that found in Oaxaca a solid and aristocratic market. This seed became the foundation for many drinks, chocolate being one of the most cherished. Its flavored captivated people's palates and today it is one of the world's favorites. Oaxacans continue grinding cocoa in a *metate* and preparing hot chocolate with water, instead of milk.

"Grandma taught me first and then my mom, we're five sisters. At twelve, we start learning everything about cooking, how to use a *metate*, a *comal*, and so on.

Among everything, what I like making most is chocolate," says Reyna Mendoza Ruiz, a traditional cook from Teotitlán del Valle. Chocolate is very representative of Teotitlán and Oaxaca; it is enjoyed for breakfast in the morning, accompanied by *panes de yema*, *pan amarillo* or *conchas* (all varieties of *pan dulce*, Mexican pastries). Reyna buys red cocoa at the Tlacolula market. She cleans the seeds, removing all the cracked ones, and soaks the rest in water. She turns the stove on and toasts them over a *comal*. When the skin darkens and the seeds pop, they are ready. Meanwhile, she places a clay bowl with hot coals under her *metate* to warm it up and, once it reaches the right temperature, she takes the cacao seeds and removes their skins.

Reyna Mendoza Ruiz

After peeling the cocoa, when the *metate* is warm enough, Reyna grabs cinnamon and begins to grind. Slowly, she adds cocoa and brown sugar. The mixture takes on a dough-like consistency that overflows into a bowl, where she kneads little cocoa balls and allows them to dry. This way, when one craves some hot chocolate, you fill a chocolate jug with hot water and a dry chocolate ball and you start whisking with a *molinillo*. "The foam is very meaningful as it represents an offering of your soul to the people," says Reyna. "Everyday we drink a cup of hot chocolate with a *pan dulce*, and at parties it is served on a platter alongside three breads: a yolk bread, a *resobado*, and a *concha*.

That's how it's usually served. If it is for a *contentada* (a meeting for an agreement or a deal between families,) ten yolk breads are served per cup," she says.

"Chocolate is very energizing, even though they say that's the reason we have diabetes, it's not true, chocolate has nothing to do with it, it had to do with the amount of sugar we consume, but chocolate doesn't have to have sugar, it's optional," argues Reyna.

Chocolate can be enjoyed all year round in Oaxaca and Teotitlán. It is common for women to make chocolate tablets for selling. Reyna says Teotitlán was the first Zapotec town of the Central Valleys and that chocolate was a drink only for kings there. "We are very honored that this continues to exist and it's a part of our everyday life. I give cooking classes on Tuesdays and Fridays. We give them here in our home. We also serve lunch and dinner for groups, but only with a reservation," Reyna concludes.

Celia Florián

144

32 Champurrado

Champurrar (verb) is to mix a liquor with another; the *champurrado* is, therefore, the result of mixing, in this case, a liquid made with corn and another made with cocoa. First, heirloom corn is sought from a local supplier, then it is husked, washed, kernels are removed, and *tlaciahual* is made. "*Tlaciahual* is the technique of cooking corn with only water, without any additives, and you don't boil the water first and then add the corn, but you heat the water along with the corn and, once boiling, you leave it there for a little while and then you try it," explains Celia Florián, a traditional cook originally from La Ciénega, Zimatlán. The corn has to be just right, that is, it must pop and look somewhat whitish, then it is taken off the heat and left to rest until the following day. "*Tlaciahual* is always made a day in advance, never on the same day, it takes time as it continues to cook in the hot water and cools down naturally," explains Celia, President and Founder of the Traditional Cooks of Oaxaca Organization.

For the drink, Celia generally uses yellow corn, although she also uses white. Once the *tlaciahual* is ready, the corn is rinsed and ground twice in a hand mill until it is very fine. Then, it is mixed well with some water inside of an *apaxtle* (a large clay pot), strained through a cheesecloth, the *chincaxtle* (fibers and corn skins) is removed and set aside on a separate container. Celia boils the remaining corn soaked water to obtain an *atole*, adds chocolate and whisks it with a *molinillo* as boils, and finishes by serving it in a clay bowl.

Champurrado is a drink that's enjoyed every morning in Oaxaca. It can be found at Las Quince Letras restaurant, where Celia Florián is a chef and owner, but also at the markets and the streets of Oaxaca early in the mornings.

María Colmenares Salvador

33

Atole de espuma

o chocolateatole

This drink is made with corn and *pinole*, composed of previously ground and toasted cocoa, cinnamon, and corn. Although there are many variations of the drink, depending on the town it's being made at.

"I learned to prepare [the drink] as a child from my mother, who learned from her own mother, so it is a recipe from generations ago. It is served during town parties, whether it's a baptism, a first communion, a wedding, it is a festive or everyday drink," says María Colmenares Salvador, originally from Zimatlán de Álvarez.

First, dry corn cobs are selected, cut, kernels taken off, and cooked, being careful not to overcook, corn kernels should not burst. The grains are then ground to obtain a dough. That dough is mixed with water and strained through a cheesecloth or napkin to make the *atole*. "Once the *atole* has been strained, the ground corn is strained inside the pot, where it will be cooked, and set over low heat to avoid sticking, and it's stirred, and stirred. You add sugar and cinnamon, and you can start seeing the *atole* thicken." The consistency should no be too watery or too thick, says Mrs. Mary.

Another part of the *chocolateatole* process is making the *pinole*, which contains corn, cocoa, and cinnamon. In a *comal*, Mrs. Mary toasts white corn until it takes on a golden hue. Then, she adds the previously washed and moist cacao and moves it around the *comal* so it doesn't burn. She toasts the cocoa, lightly toasts the cinnamon, and both ingredients are then ground in a *metate* to prepare the *pinole*. *Pinole* is mixed with cold water. Then, with a *molinillo*, Mrs. Mary whisks the liquid until it foams.

In Zimatlán, the hot *atole* is first poured inside of a clay cup, then the foam is added on top and served accompanied by an *alcahuete* (wooden stick for stirring).

Atole de espuma is served for breakfast alongside two pieces of bread. In Zimatlán, it is sold at the Molino de San Antonio, which Mrs. Mary recommends.

34
Sombra
Mezcal Artesanal

Mezcal is one of the most emblematic distilled liquors of Mexico and Oaxaca. The word *mezcal* originates from *mescal* or *mexcal*, itself coming from *me-xcalli*, made up of *metl* "maguey," and *xcalli* or *ixcalli* "cooked" or "boiled," therefore meaning "cooked or boiled maguey." This is how indigenous peoples called the roasted "heads" of certain sweet-tasting magueys that are still sold in some markets today. Currently though, the word is used more in relation to the liquor made from fermented roasted "heads" of various agaves.

Making *mezcal* requires a commitment to the product but, above all, to the environment and the community, as the plant is not like others that have to reach maturity to be used. Once the maguey ripens it has to die in order to share its gift, which is why at Sombra Mezcal Artesanal, they make an effort to to produce a sustainable mezcal, promoting ecological business models.

In Santiago Matatlán, a town near the old Zapotec city of Mitla, Sombra's *palenque* (an artisanal agave distillery) is surprising for its cleanliness, neatness, and factory structure, but also for their social responsibility.

To make *mezcal*, the first step is to harvest the agaves. There is a meticulous process to identify each plant's age because, depending on their gender and ripeness, its sweetness can vary, so waiting until they are at their prime is essential for optimal results. You must wait between seven and twenty-six years, depending on the species of agave in question.

In the fields, the *pencas* (heads) are cut to get the *piñas* ("pineapples" or cores) of the magueys. Once you have a good enough quantity, they are sent to the *palenque*. There, they are cooked inside of a stone oven, which is a huge cone-shaped hole in the field or yard of the *palenque*, that is heated to 900-1,100 degrees Celsius. Maguey fibers or *bagasse* is spread over the stones, then the pineapples are stacked on top, and it is covered with tarpaulins and dirt to hermetically seal the oven, preventing steam from escaping. For this process, Sombra uses certified oak wood, which they buy directly from local woodcutters who reforest in order to maintain the ecosystems. Once the magueys have been cooked, they are chopped into pieces and transferred to the *tahona* (a large stone wheel used to mash the roasted agave, usually pulled by a donkey or horse) for grinding. They don't use a "beast," and the more traditional horse, mule or donkey is replaced here with an electric car that pulls the mill stone around the axis, making the process faster and friendlier, eschewing use and abuse of draught animals.

The ground agave is then transferred to the fermentation vats and the resulting liquid will be directly moved to the still for distillation, which will take between five or six hours. "About eighteen percent of the alcoholic content results from the first distillation, it's already clear, and what comes out is a liquid called ordinary, which has eighteen percent of alcohol content. Then you distill it again, you remove the spirit, you remove the alcohol and leave the water underneath. That can already be called *mezcal*; following the second distillation you can start calling it *mezcal* and it's around 57 proof," says José Pablo Raña Zorilla, a chemist in charge of the process. Although, at other *palenques* they light firewood to distill using copper stills, at Sombra they use propane gas with an air mixer. "You can reach 99%, 100% of the gas [that] you burn is transformed into energy, meaning there's no waste, and the propane we use is transformed into heat. All the lights, pumps, everything runs with the same energy that we put back into the electricity grid," says Pablo, who also refines the flavor and sensory profiles of the *mezcal*.

Sombra also manufactures bricks. During the production of *mezcal* they obtain *vinasse*, which is the residual liquid from the first distillation. This is placed in containers for the production of adobe bricks.

Sombra's adobes are made of dirt, maguey *bagasse*, and *vinasse*. Nothing goes to waste, as *bagasse* is the fiber that helps compacting the bricks. Other *palenques* use their waste as fertilizer, but most of them discard it, polluting fields and rivers. This *palenque* tries to promote recycling waste by talking to other types of manufacturers. Currently, they manufacture up to 250 adobe bricks per day when *mezcal* production is high. These bricks are donated to communities in the Sierra Mixe, which have been used to build 16 houses in Zacatepec Mixe in conjunction with the Alfredo Harp Helú Foundation, along with three other houses in Ayutla, and a donation for another house in the Isthmus.

Once the *mezcal* is ready, it is transferred to cooling tubs that use rainwater collected for that very purpose. The liquid is then completely stabilized and ready to be packaged and enjoyed.

35

Tejate de maíz abierto

Tejate is a drink that has many variations and diverse interpretations. In Teotitlán del Valle they prepare *tejate de maíz abierto*, whose name implies the use of "open corn," as it has in its elaboration process a technique that separates it from the more popular and foamy variation of the drink. "I learned at the age of eight because my mother taught me and we could say it's an everyday drink. It is made with corn, with *cuanextle*, just the ashes, and it is crispy as the corn is cooked. After the *cuanextle*, it is rinsed well and you start cooking it for about four or five hours over the fire until the corn bursts, and once open you allow it to rest overnight and the following day you make the *tejate*," explains Abigail Mendoza Ruiz, a traditional cook from Teotitlán del Valle.

The corn is placed inside the *cuanextle* (a technique of cooking corn with ashes) and it is cooled down after boiling. Knowing its exact cooking point is essential so the beverage has the right amount of thickness. After one day, it is rinsed and ground in a *metate*. "You have to make sure all the skins are removed since it makes a big difference in ensuring the corn cooks beautifully. If you don't remove the skins the corn cannot be used for making *maíz abierto*," says Abigail.

Abigail Mendoza Ruiz

The dough is placed in an *apaxtle* (clay dish) where it is mixed together by hand. "You have to do it slowly to avoid small balls of *masa* from forming, and since it is sticky you can end up with large balls, so you must do it little by little, and you add water so it all dissolves are you mix," adds Abigail who, in addition to being a cook, is a wool rug weaver, an artisanal tradition characteristic of her town. You can use any type of corn, it can be white, yellow, or blue, but it must be dry. Abigail and her sisters use corn from their own harvest. The characteristics of their *milpa* define the drink they make. In Oaxaca, many types of corn are specifically grown for certain dishes and planting different varieties also helps prevent their shortage, given that some types of corn do not tolerate pests or climate change, while others do. These parcels are the result of enormous wisdom, as they avoid famine at all costs. Abigail Mendoza Ruiz is the most famous traditional cook in Oaxaca and Mexico. She inherited her culinary knowledge from her mother and the art of wool weaving, dyeing, and designing from her father. "There's a lot to know about drinks, because there are many *tejates*: there's *tejate* with *chile*, there's sweet *tejate*, and there are *tejate* varieties like there are *atoles*.

The fundamental basis of a traditional kitchen is only grinding using a the *metate*, nothing else because the flavors won't be the same. We have to conserve this, make sure that all people and the younger generations, which is what I'm trying to do, continue cooking this way," says Abigail with a beautiful smile. Abigail and her five sisters know how to cook and have transmitted their ancestral wisdom to their daughters and sons. The Mendoza family saveguards traditional Oaxacan cuisine, disseminating methods and techniques with the younger generations by promoting the art of grinding in a *metate* and preparing food with love. Tlamanalli restaurant has been serving their culinary delights for 29 years and its located on Avenida Juárez 39 in Teotitlán del Valle.

Graciela & Édgar Ángeles Carreño

36

Mezcal

Real Minero

A *maestra* or *maestro mezcalero* (*mezcal* master) is not just that who makes *mezcal*, but that who lives and shares that ancestral culture. Anyone who knows the elaboration process of *mezcal* can produce it, but a *maestro mezcale*ro is, above all, someone who merges and proposes a way of understanding and assuming life through the beverage. If a *mezcal* is linked to a community, a family, or both, it's common for the beverage to express itself in line with that reality.

Real Minero *Mezcal* is a family business in Santa Catarina Minas, nearby the town of Ocotlán, in the Central Valleys of Oaxaca. It's a seventeen-year-old brand, though the project begun four generations ago. At the beginning, four decades ago, the production of *mezcal* was carried out in collective community spaces, when Mr. Lorenzo Ángeles Mendoza bought a *palenque* that they named "La Concepción." Since then, Real Minero *Mezcal* has functioned independently. "The project is carried out by the children; my father passes away. In December it will be three years since he died. The project continues through my mother, Candelaria Carreño Pérez, my brother, Edgar Ángeles Carreño, Adriana, Miryam, Elvia, and myself. We are seven children and five of us work on this project, each one participating in a different way," says Graciela Ángeles Carreño, leader of the project, a position her father assigned her with.

Edgar Ángeles Carreño is the *maestro mezcalero* and production manager, while Adriana is in charge of administration, and Miryam and Elvia handle sales. They all work in the family business wishing for their *mezcal* and project to succeed, which is broader than just a liquor brand.

Real Minero *Mezcal* is commited to social and ecological responsibility, two principles that lead to two projects: The El Rosario library —focused on educating young people particularly from the community— and Project LAM, which honors Mr. Lorenzo Ángeles Mendoza, who always showed great interest in agaves and the cultivation of different varieties.

Project LAM looks to address ecological responsibility. "We not only think about the need to plant and reproduce maguyes, but also about understanding that agaves are a part of a habitat and within that habitat there are animals, plants, and also humans. For that reason, when you talk about maguey sustainability, you have to think about water, firewood, agaves, but also food," says Graciela, referring to the fact that in recent years *mezcal* demand has driven many farmers to agave production, leaving behind food agriculture.

Project LAM also focuses on educating and sharing the research of *mezcal* producers with interested people in a language that's accessible to all. Graciela Ángeles explains that, "we propose showing this part of applied science stating that we are not a research institute, we are not academics, we are not formal scientists, but we all generate knowledge." The project's activities include germinating agave seeds naturally, eschewing chemical processes or industrialized technology. On top of that, Project LAM does interpretive hiking in a five-season agave garden where they talk about the plant's reproduction with mainly children, young people, and those interested in the subject. "This has allowed us to talk to children of various ages, as young as preschoolers. It is a beautiful thing since it allows you to talk about so many things, it allows you to make children aware of the importance of nature and how reproduction works for humans, plants, and animals. Agaves don't grow in just one place or only in flat places,

some like to live in very extreme conditions, on rocks, on slopes," says Graciela. Mother plants are planted on the interpretative path so that they can produce floral scape, pollination, and generate seeds to reestablish reproduction and conservation of several agave varieties. The agave life cycle is documented for research purposes, from seed germination to sowing. "It's great having a high germination percentage and it opens a dialogue of whether cloning agaves is necessary to grow them in significant quantities. Through these records, we have data showing that an agave can leave ten thousand, fifteen thousand, and twenty thousand seeds."

Project LAM's efforts are financed through *mezcal* production and independently from any political or government institution. Also, through these means, seed sowing and seedling care of up to three leaves are carried out in order to transfer them to a nursery for nine and twelve months before transplanting them to the fields.

The whole process is closely monitored and photographed by biologist Matías Domínguez Laso. "We have captured two bat species, and our hypothesis is that some agaves are not pollinated by bats but by insects such as moths, bees, or nocturnal butterflies, and these are things that open new paths; suddenly, it became common [opinion] that the universal agave pollinator is the bat and it appears it might not be so," says Graciela.

Real Minero produces a range of fourteen *mezcales* from various agaves. The brand can be purchased in Oaxaca City's historic downtown at the store La Casa Grande, stand 14, within Casa Murguía. In addition, interested people can visit Project LAM or Real Minero *palenque* in Minas. The tour lasts three hours and you can learn a lot about the maguey plant and the delicious drink that emanates from it.

Josefina Elba Cruz Sumano

37

Agua de támala

A *támala* is a beautiful pumpkin, also called *tamaloya*, whose name comes from *tamal* and *ayotli*. That is, *tamalli*, "tamal," and *ayotli*, "pumpkin," meaning "pumpkin as *tamal*." It is a large, round pumpkin whose flesh has the consistency of a *tamal*. Pumpkins are exclusive to the American continent and there are about fifteen species, one of which is the *támala*, known elsewhere as castile pumpkin. Its culinary uses include desserts, beverages, and some dishes.

"Since I was very young it was prepared in my town, but it is almost exclusively a seasonal drink from late November, December, or early January. It was prepared for those working the fields during corn harvest," says Josefina Elba Cruz Sumano, originally from San Juan Chilateca, Ocotlán, who learned how to make this drink from her mother and grandmother. It all begins at the *milpa*, when Elba sees a ripe pumpkin, picks it up, washes and slices it into small pieces to cook with brown sugar and cinnamon. "It's cooked until it is very soft, and once cooked you remove the seeds, then once it's very soft you remove it from the heat, and it's allowed to cool down overnight so the following day you can prepare it by removing the skin," explains Elba, a traditional cook from Oaxaca.

She makes her *nixtamal* with *cacahuazintle* corn. "Once the *nixtamal* is cooked and cold, it is washed thoroughly until it turns white, and then you boil it once more until it bursts so it's very soft." The following day, she beats the *támala* flesh to get a mixture of light consistency, serves it in a *jícara* and adds the popped corn to enjoy it. *Agua de támala* is sweet and refreshing, and it is enjoyed along with food or when it's hot outside.

It is typical of harvest months. It is an orange drink with *pozole* corn on top, a unique combination.

Cibeles Ramírez Colmenares & María Colmenares Salvador

38
Calabaza batida

Calabaza batida is one of the most traditional drinks of Zimatlán de Álvarez, Zaachila, Ocotlán, as well as the rest of the Central Valleys. It is seasonal, of harvesting season, of the *milpa*, of when the corn and the pumpkins are green and tender, though the type of pumpkin can vary depending on the area or season.

Pumpkins are annual plants that belong to a very large family, which include chayote, *acocote*, and even *bules*, exclusive to the American continent. There are about fifteen species of pumpkins, they are creeping, climbing, and bush plants, which contributes a lot to the *milpa*. They were domesticated about eight thousand years ago. Worldwide they are basically thought of as vegetables, but in Oaxaca they can also belong in an agua fresca.

Mrs. María Colmenares Salvador and her daughter, Cibeles Ramírez Colmenares, traditional cooks, remove the husks and chop their corn, wash and chop the pumpkins into six pieces each. "We place the ingredients in a large pot half-full with water: pumpkin, corn, then *panela* and some cinnamon sticks. We also have three cobs of corn for grinding and, at the end, when the pumpkin and corn are cooked, we take the kernels off the cobs, grind them, and rinse them with water," explains Mrs. Mary.

The grains are ground in the *metate*, water is added to the *masa*, and it is strained through a cheesecloth, in which the *atole* is also strained, decanting the grain *bagasse*. The liquid from the corn is poured into a *jícara* and, at the same time, corn husks are placed at the bottom of a clay pot to avoid the ingredients from sticking to it.

Once the pot is ready, Cibeles crushes the ingredients with a *molinillo* to break them apart and thicken the drink. "When the pumpkin is completely dissolved and mixed with the corn, the already strained and ground corn is added in," says Mrs. Mary, who learned to prepare the drink from her mother, an inheritance that she is now transmitting to her own daughter, Cibeles.

The drink is ready after two hours of cooking. It is constantly whisked to prevent it from sticking to the pot. "I remember that, as a child, we used to drink this beverage during corn season; my grandfather used to bring the harvest and my grandmother would prepare it. She had us husk the corn and she would cook everything, always using clay pots. Bringing lots of corn and pumpkins turned into a party and she would have us take the kernels off," shares Cibeles. *Calabaza batida* is usually enjoyed during the afternoon as supper, with only corn. Its thickness is of light consistency and sweet taste, without being too rich. It is only prepared in homes, so it can't be found for sale as it is a family drink. Cibeles and her mother work at organizing banquets where they promote Oaxacan cuisine. "We grew up selling food, my mom made stuffed peppers and we sold them to the neighbors. At 23 I started traveling to share Oaxacan food and my mother keeps the soul in the company. All those who came to work with us, whether chefs, cooks, helpers, etc. would learn from roasting a tomato to what the exact point for *nixtamal* is. She is in the kitchen and I am in sales and event design," shares Cibeles.

39

Café de olla

María del Pilar Cabrera Arroyo

Café de olla is an emblematic Mexican drink that is enjoyed on a daily basis in several parts of the country. It is common to make this drink to start your day refreshed, especially for breakfast, as it accompanies traditional food of the country well. Many families use clay pots, others use enamel jugs, but these are generally tools of yesteryear. In Oaxaca though, the clay pot is essential.

Café de olla is closely linked with breakfast that, in Mexico, is copious and splendid, to start the day well. Which is why a hot *café de olla*, served in a clay cup, helps you wake up and warms your hands and soul. It has the sweetness you seek for and enough spices to enrich your day with its flavor notes. *Café de olla* usually reminds you of family, of home. The cook, María del Pilar Cabrera Arroyo, prepares *café de olla* just like the one her grandmother used to make her. The coffee was roasted on a *comal* and a clay pot was used for its elaboration. "For me, *café de olla* is like a black *mole*, isn't it? Each person has their own mix. There are some who add fresh orange peel. What we do is dehydrate the orange peel, mix it with anise, cinnamon, cloves, and allspice to give it a more aromatic touch," says María del Pilar. There are many versions of *café de olla*, but the most common has coffee, brown sugar, and cinnamon, but there are those who add more ingredients for a different flavor.

To make this drink, Pilar roasts the spices, then transfers them to the clay pot and adds brown sugar and dehydrated orange. Once it boils, it is allowed to rest and then served in a clay cup.

The *café de olla* that Pilar prepares stands out for its flavor combination, and it not only tastes like cinnamon and *panela* or *piloncillo*, but the sweetness of the anise along with the orange and allspice create a unique taste that can be enjoyed in the mornings or afternoons.

Pilar Cabrera studied food engineering, but is currently the owner and chef of the restaurant La Olla, in Oaxaca City, which specializes in Oaxacan food. In addition, during her spare time, she teaches cooking classes for people with or without culinary skills. "Almost all menus have a famous *mole*, there is one called *amarillo*, or *verde*. The one that's 100 percent Oaxaca is the *chichilo*. And when it's *chicatana* (flying ants) season, there's *salsa de chicatana*. Almost all are five-course menus, from appetizer to finish, and we end with a *mezcal* tasting," explains Pilar.

175

Sierra Norte

This region is located in northern Oaxaca and borders with six of the eight major regions comprising the state. To the north, it borders with the state of Puebla and the regions of Papaloapan and Cañada; to the south with the Central Valleys, Sierra Sur, and the Isthmus; to the west with the Central Valleys, Sierra Sur, and the Coast; to the northwest with the Papaloapan region, and to the east with another area of the Central Valleys, the Mixteca, and the Cañada. It has sixty-eight municipalities and three districts: Ixtlán, Villa Alta, and Zacatepec or Mixe. Its name comes from the mountainous area of the Sierra Madre de Oaxaca, located north of the state, which incudes the Sierra Juárez, Sierra Mixe, and Sierra Mazateca. It is considered one of the most biodiverse areas in the world. It makes-up thirteen percent of the state's territory.

The Sierra Norte, which reaches even the skirts of the Pico de Orizaba, is also called Sierra Oaxaqueña or Sierra de Oaxaca. The weather is continuously rainy and is, in fact, the region of the state where it rains the most, which makes the territory rich in flora and fauna. As an example, in the border with Huautla de Jiménez, trees such as oak, rosewood, ironwood, *palo santo*, and pine grow — woods that drive a cuisine that imprints their hot beverages with unique flavors. On the way to the region towards the southwest, around Cuicatlán, among the rivers and mountains between Oaxaca and Tuxtepec, the fauna is brimming with little spotted cats, deer, jaguars, among other animals, while, near the Papaloapan region snakes abound. Towards Ixtlán there are many rivers that thicken the Papaloapan, a landscape that produced many dishes to complement the beverages of the region.

In many towns of the Sierra Norte, which are often humid and cold, it is common to find an important wealth of fruit trees such as apricot, apple, peach, pear, and quince —main ingredients for many *aguas frescas*. Although the Sierra Norte has many cold towns exceeding 3,300 meters above sea level, there are others at only 1,000 meters above sea level with warmer temperatures that are conducive to more tropical vegetation and delicious fruits such as mangoes, bananas, and sugarcane. On the other hand, in between them, at 2,500 meters above sea level, we find Tlahuitoltepec, with a temperate climate as well as cold and cloudy seasons that allow pines, *ocotes*, and oak trees to grow, which also lead to the making of rich and diverse drinks.

The list of drinks that can be enjoyed in the area encompass a multitude of options because of the region's microclimates, delighting those who've been preparing them for millennia in a range of extraordinary colors and flavors.

40
Pinole

The word *pinole* comes from the Nahuatl *pinol* and *atl*, "roasted corn water," which was originally how this pre-Hispanic drink was consumed before evolving into different variations over time, such as the very common roasted cornmeal that's sweetened with *piloncillo* and mixed with cinnamon, and as the frothy cocoa drink from Oaxaca that delights many.

45 kilometers north of Oaxaca City is Santa Catarina Ixtepeji. As you arrive to the town, pine began adorning the landscape as the air turns cold, since the area is at an altitude of more than 1,800 meters above sea level and it's surrounded by mountains. There, Elisa León Pérez makes *pinole*. "I learned how to make it from my grandmothers and my mother. And one learns through play and practice. My grandmother had her *metate*, and she would begin making it there, starting with roasting the corn," says Elisa.

Although neither cinnamon nor sugar are of pre-Hispanic origin, this recipe clearly has ancestral roots, and both its reddish foam and the celebrations in which it is present show its ceremonial origins.

Elisa León Pérez

First, white corn cobs are selected, which must be the largest in size. Then, the corn is placed on a *comal*, to which ash is added. "The bread is made with firewood, that ash is then sifted until it's fine, very fine, and then it's spread on top of the corn for roasting over low heat." The corn is roasted until "it's at the right point," and from there it goes through two different filters: one to remove the excess ash and the other to remove the skins through an *ixtle sack*. "Since it's already been roasted, the skins aren't needed anymore, and the ash will help remove all that," explains Elisa.

After the corn, it's time to roast the cocoa beans. They are done separately to prevent them from burning. Once both the beans and the corn are ready, they are placed on the *metate* for grinding. After the first grinding, a little cinnamon and *achiote* are added before grinding until it is "very fine." This mixture is then transferred to the *cajete de gabil* (a round and deep bowl used for foaming), to which a little cold water and sugar are added. This powder is whisked with a *molinillo* to obtain an abundant amount of red foam.

At the same time, a white *atole* is made with corn selected for this purpose. The corn kernels are cooked until boiling. Once boiled, it is ground in the *metate* and dissolved in water as it is strained. It is boiled once again, adding sugar and cinnamon. The *pinole* is added to this base.

The delicious drink takes almost a whole work day to prepare. It is common to find it at weddings, baptisms, and festivities, although it can also be enjoyed daily for breakfast along with chocolate, *pan de manteca*, or *marquesotes* (another bread from certain regions of Oaxaca).

41

In Mexico, there are several ceremonial drinks that are linked with complex cultural systems, themselves linked with ancestral pre-Hispanic worldviews. Some of them are alcoholic and are prepared only for rituals and offerings. One of them is the *tepache con rojo*, which is sacred to the Mixes or *Ayuujk jää'y* ("people of the florid or elevated word" or "those who go to the hill"), an ancient community in northwestern Oaxaca who proudly refer to themselves as the "never conquered." In order to make *tepache con rojo*, it is essential to hike the sacred Zempoaltépetl or Cempoaltépetl mountain, whose Nahuatl name means "twenty hills," a number related to their vigesimal numeral system. This majestic mountain, mysterious and sacred, contains among its several elevations what is the highest peak for the Mixes. It is where the earth and the sky come together to become one, a site of major importance to the *Ayuujk jää'y*; a natural, cosmic lookout where energies conducive to animal, plant, and food offerings are found; a ceremonial center for asking forgiveness from the creator, gratitude, offerings, as well as requests for work, health, or personal, family, or community wellbeing.

Tepache con rojo

María Díaz Cortés & Juana Gallardo Jiménez

There, *Nääx Tääk*, "Mother Earth," is worshiped. They believe the legendary character and king of the Mixes, *konk ëy*, "good king," also called *Konk tëy*, "burned king," was born from the Zempoaltépetl's insides. It is the sacred mountain of supply and fertility, it is an energy and deity in itself that gives life meaning and belonging to the *Ayuujk jää'y*. Since this is a sacred drink, it must follow an elaboration ritual: "If I make the *tepache* it means that I went and returned from the sacred Zempoaltépetl mountain. If I don't go to the mountain, I can't make the *tepache*," says María del Carmen Vázquez Díaz. It is a sacred drink for the ritual ascent, necessary to get to the top of the Zempoaltépetl and

to the altar of stones standing before a deep abyss that expands to the coastal plains of the Gulf —a landscape lost beneath an immense ocean of white clouds.

For Mixes, the ritual of hiking the mountain means a meeting with the mountain and the entities dwelling there. In Santa María Tlahuitoltepec, when families have patron saint parties or similar celebrations, or just a life event that calls for a climb, they make *tepache con rojo*, which gives them the strength to ascent. In addition to the *tepache*, it is necessary to bring an offering in order to climb the mountain.

181

This offering is decided by the *xëmaapyë* or ritual specialist, a wise person who provides guidance on the things and quantities that must be offered depending on the type of ritual or "encounter with the root." The main offerings brought to the mountain are: *elaborado de masa "xätxy," tamales, tortillas* with a *chile* spread, *envuelto de hierba santa,* poultry, *mezcal,* cigarettes to ward off evil, flowers to perfume the soul and for happiness, among other gifts. When María del Carmen and her grandfather Agustín Díaz Núñez, 86, ascend to the sacred mountain, it takes approximately three hours; then, the descent takes about two hours, considering that it takes an hour to get from Tlahuitoltepec to the bottom of the mountain by car. While going uphill, it is customary to share everything that's being offered with those descending until you are left with nothing, creating a virtuous cycle between those who come and go.

At the top is the stone altar for *Konk ëy,* "good king," with remains from past offerings such as ashes, blood of slaughtered animals, food, candles, poultry feathers, and coins. Right there, Mr. Agustín spills three drops of *tepache* on the earth and prays in Mixe, asking for health and well-being. "The first drop represents gratitude for mother nature, the second drop represents gratitude for God, and the third drop is gratitude for king *Konk ëy,* who is our supreme, righteous, and wise king —a Mixe idol that is part of our lives in the past, present, and who will continue to influence our future," explains María del Carmen.

Once prayers are done, they have breakfast over some stones: some *tortillas* with a red *chile* spread and hard boiled eggs, fog surrounds everything. Then, Mr. Agustín says thanks in Mixe and the *tepache* of abundant red foam is sampled. *Pulque* (fermented agave sap drink) is used to make this *tepache,* which is bought from the *pulqueros* (*pulque* makers) in the center of town or ordered if it is to be prepared in large quantities. Water and *pulque* are added in the same proportions into a clay pot. Then, *panela* or *piloncillo* are added and allowed to ferment inside the pot.

Fermentation time depends on the person who is preparing the drink. "With some people it ferments after a day and with others even after three or four days it still hasn't fermented," says María del Carmen. The longer the fermentation lasts, the more alcoholic the drink.

There are two types of *tepache* in Tlahuitoltepec: the simple and the ritual. The latter is served with red foam. *Tepache con rojo* should only be made if the request includes a mass or when someone reaches the top of the Zempoaltépetl mountain. To get the red foam, a powder is made by grinding corn, cocoa, and *achiote.* María Díaz Cortés and Juana Gallardo Jiménez, mother and grandmother of María del Carmen, are in charge of preparing the *tepache* in the family.

After lighting the wood-burning stove, Mrs. María Díaz carefully and slowly roasts the heirloom corn in a *comal,* stirring with a wooden spoon to maintain a uniform roast, making sure not all the corn bursts. Then she repeats the same process with the cocoa and the *achiote,* only faster to prevent them from burning.

Juana Gallardo selects the cocoa and, while doing so, she teaches her great-granddaughter, Delia Mayte Vázquez Orozco, to count the beans in Mixe. Once everything is roasted, Mrs. María Díaz covers the *piloncillo* with a cloth napkin and hits it against the *metate* with the *metlapil* or hand of the *metate* (pestle) to crush it as much as possible. Once its broken apart, she delivers it to her grandmother, who grinds it in the *metate* along with the cocoa and the *achiote* to obtain a very fine powder that is then placed inside of a clay container filled with water, where it is allowed to rest for a day to give the foam a homogenous consistency.

To serve the drink, the red liquid is foamed with a *molinillo* and a wooden spoon and, finally, poured over the *tepache*. Before it can be enjoyed, words of gratefulness are shared along with the reasons why the beverage is being offered, offering three drops to the earth as well, which represent the strength and union of the Mixes and their gratitude to Mother Earth, God, and king *Konk ëy*.

During celebrations, the tradition is to drink simple *tepache* along with a delicious Mixe broth —a chicken broth with green beans, *chayotes*, and other vegetables— accompanied by yellow *mole* and bean *tamales*. Then, the *tepache con rojo*, "the one that perfumes and adds aroma to life," is presented. Afterwards, the "principal," the person who has organized the celebration, addresses his guests to say thank you and the reason for the invitation. In response, one of the guests reiterates the request made by the "principal," affirming the belief that everything that's been requested will be granted. The *tepache con rojo* should be finished during the celebration. However, if there's some left, it is distributed amongst the guests to prevent it from going bad, which would be disrespectful to king *Konk ëy*.

All of this takes place in Tlahuitoltepec, in the Sierra Norte of Oaxaca, two and a half hours away from the state capital, in a town unique for its people, climate, food, and geography, whose forest vegetation creates a fresh and nice environment year-round.

Luciana Pérez Vázquez

42

Pulque de
Tlahuitoltepec

The agave or *maguey* is a plant belonging to a huge family. There are many verities and some of them make *pulque*. For a plant to work for *pulque* production, it much be full grown after eight or ten years, depending on the type of maguey. Early in the morning, Luciana Pérez Vázquez begins working, which she started learning at the age of five, when she would help her parents extract *aguamiel* (a type of mead) to make *pulque*.

"One's work has to be real, you have to love what you do," says Luciana, originally from the town of San Antonio Tejas, a ranch in Santa María Tlahuitoltepec, a municipality of the Sierra Mixe. It all begins with a climb to the hills to search for *magueys*, a difficult task as the environment is foggy and humid and the landscape steep and slippery. Luciana is quick and confident as she is well acquainted with the land. She does this twice a day. In the morning, she climbs a hill thirty minutes behind her house and, in the afternoon, she walks to a different one for an hour and a half.

Once she gets to the magueys, she arranges her stuff on the floor and starts extracting the *aguamiel* from within the plant's heart. "My mother planted this maguey," she explains, pointing to a very large plant.

The extraction process takes approximately two hours since the plant has to be located, cleaned, and then extract and store the *aguamiel* she'll take home. "There, I go get *aguamiel* every morning. My conscience got it slowly. I have to do it, but I didn't like it as a child." And just like her mother taught her, Luciana teaches her son and her three daughters who help out with everything.

After extracting the sweet liquid from the plant, its core must be prepared to promote new *aguamiel* to accumulate, for which a piece is cut and scraped clean with a jicara. Then, the heart of the plant is covered to protect it from the rain and prevent animals from drinking the liquid or damaging it. With great care she tried not to completely cover that part of the plant so it can breathe.

Traditionally, an *acocote* (calabash or bottle gourd) for the *aguamiel* extraction, but Luciana uses a recycled plastic bottle, which must be very clean as any impurity can spoil the delicate drink. In this way, she can extract up to seven liters a day from about seven magueys.

In addition to taking care of the maguey's heart, it is important to remove and prune the weeds growing around the agave, otherwise it can use up the fertilizer and nutrients of the plant.

The remoteness of the hill she must climb up to in the afternoon delays the work. After a bit more than an hour, Luciana teams up with her son. He's in charge of extracting the *aguamiel* and bottling it, while she cleans and readies the plant. Once the daily *aguamiel* has been gathered, they descend from the hill and head home to prepare the *pulque*.

The *aguamiel* is placed inside of a clay pot to which she adds a piece of *palo de timbre* (plant, *Acaciella angustissima*), which accelerates fermentation. The amount of sticks added depends on the consistency of the liquid. During the process, Luciana knows when to add more.

The *palo de timbre* has to be cleaned and washed well a week before use. Once it successfully ferments the drink it is used as fertilizer. A good *pulque* needs at least one hour of fermentation. It can be enjoyed after that time, but the longer it's fermented, the more alcohol it will have.

Since the cool climate of San Antonio Tejas is helpful to this process, the pot is placed outside to avoid heat and allow for cool drafts of air, which will produce a higher quality *pulque*.

In Tlahuitoltepec, there are about eight people who work in *aguamiel* extraction to make *pulque*, which they sell in the center of town, where people enjoy it served in *jicaras*.

Francisca Bautista & Rosalba Aquino Bautista

43

Pozontle

Villa Hidalgo Yalalag is just over three hours away from Oaxaca City. The town's most representative drink is the *pozontle*, made with *cacahuacintle* or *pozolero*, a corn that looks like foam when it bursts, hence its name, which comes from Nahuatl *pozol*, "foam." "We drink it during patron saint celebrations, weddings, harvest, we always have some *pozontle* ready here," says Francisca Bautista, who learned how to make the drink from her grandmothers more than eighteen years ago. "For about fifteen years, I was here in the center of Villa Hidalgo town selling, and now I've been traveling to Oaxaca with the *pozontle*," she explains.

Currently, Rosalba Aquino Bautista, Francisca's daughter, also makes a living out of preparing and selling this drink. "I learned when I was about fifteen years old. I've always helped my mother, since I was little, but at fifteen I started grinding in a *metate*," says Rosalba. To prepare the *pozontle*, heirloom corn is nixtamalized with ashes. A Oaxacan technique called *necuanextle* is employed, where wood ashes are used instead of lime, in this case from oak. After nixtamalization, the corn is allowed to rest overnight. The following day, it is boiled, washed, and soaked in water once again until it begins to bloom like a flower, after approximately five hours. Then it is transferred to a *metate* for grinding.

The cocoa is also washed, dried outside for three or four days, depending on the sun's intensity, and gently roasted so it is easier for Francisca and Rosalba to grind in a *metate*. Then, they add the sap of the *cocolmeca* plant, removing its *bagasse* for a very fine grind.

"Once this is done small balls start forming and these are dissolved in a *jícara*, *panela* water is added as well as corn kernels, and it is whisked until it's frothy with a *molinillo*," explains Rosalba. The steps for serving the drink are: water, the cocoa ball that is dissolved by hand or with the *molinillo*, foaming and, finally, adding the kernels.

Enriqueta Contreras Contreras

44

Té de
poleo

Poleo de monte is a wild, semi-bush herb with a minty smell that makes many people think it belongs to the mint family. However, it can also be called "herb of the drunk," *Satureja laevigata,* as drinking it in a tea helps those who suffer from a hangover. It is one of those plants that oscillates between the world of food and medicine. The plant grows in the forest and the mountains of Oaxaca. It is a sacred plant for the Zapotecs and used for celebrations and as an offering for guests.

"It is also used ground for beans. We make bean *tamales* with *poleo* leaves and we can also make *poleo* tea for digestion or stomach cramps, it's an antibiotic. It is a sacred plant at the main altars, when someone goes to ask for a woman's hand or when there's a wedding, it is what they offer, a natural gift for all the guests," explains Mrs. Enriqueta Contreras Contreras, better known as Doña Queta.

Doña Queta is Zapotec, from the Benito Juárez community in the Sierra Norte. "I speak Zapotec from the Sierra Juárez, I am 81 years old and I have dedicated myself to traditional medicine since I was a child. I've been a midwife since the age of seventeen," says Doña Queta.

Currently, she and her daughter give massages, healing cleanses, *temazcal* baths (a healing sweat lodge) flower baths, postprandial baths, as well as making products with medicinal plants such as syrups, tinctures, soaps, microdoses, and other traditional remedies. People seek her to cure their physical and emotional ills because of her wisdom and knowledge of plants and their properties.

Poleo tea can be prepared with the fresh or dried plant. To make her tea, Doña Queta makes a roll with the leaves and stems of the plant, immerses them in a clay pot filled with boiling water for ten minutes, removes from heat and serves hot. The mint aroma fills the entire kitchen; it is so pleasant that it invites you to enjoy a cup of tea at any time of day.

"Many people drink it with some honey, and if you have an upset stomach you can add a pinch of salt. Whether fresh or dried the properties are the same," says Doña Queta.

She belongs to the third generation of healers in her town. "Being a healer is no easy task, it means knowing yourself as a person and knowing the people you're going to take care of. There's also a sense of responsibility, understanding human pain, feeling the pain of others to know how to solve their health concerns." Her granddaughter has started learning about plants, which means five generations of her family will have this wisdom.

Knowledge of herbalism is still very present in various towns of Oaxaca. The parts of the plant such as leaves, stem, flowers, and root have different medicinal properties. This is why Doña Queta urges people to take care of the environment. "It is unfortunate and sad how everything is being destroyed instead of building love for life and nature. It is very difficult at this point. People don't understand the damage that is being done to mother earth and to the elements like water. Once they hit bottom it will already be too late," she says.

197

Costa

This is the southernmost region of Oaxaca and it is located along the Pacific Ocean, bordering with two of the state's eight regions. To the north it borders with the Sierra Sur; to the south with the Pacific Ocean; to the east with the Isthmus of Tehuantepec, and to the west with the state of Guerrero. It constitutes 11 percent of Oaxaca's territory. It has 50 municipalities and three districts: Jamiltepec, Juquila, and Pochutla. The Coast is characterized by its wet climate, because of the large amount of rivers found in the region that come from the Sierra Madre del Sur. Meanwhile, at its front is the ocean, providing the people with immense wealth because of its lagoons and mangroves, along with the incredible amount of seafood available. Walking around the area's roads, cars loaded with sesame seeds or peanuts from the coastal plains stand out. The fauna is lavish and animals such as tapir, weasel, otter, shrew, marten, ounce, anteater, raccoon, porcupine, eagle, rattlesnake, iguana, and chameleon can be found, among others. Agriculture and fishing are two of the most important economic activities, with the production of Pluma coffee from Pluma Hidalgo, Pochutla, stands out.

The area is also known for their lemon crops, used to produce essential oils, as well as for their coconut palm, fine woods, tropical species, livestock, and mining. The sea salt from the south of Pinotepa Nacional and Río Grande is famous for being produced by hand. This region is also famous for its sulfur waters such as those found in Atotonilco, Juquila, and La Cañada de Minas, to name a few. But it is especially well known for its beaches and touristic environment, among which are Puerto Escondido, Puerto Ángel, and Huatulco, as well as the religious center of Santa Catarina Juquila.

45

Curaditos

Cirina Leyva Vera

Doña Ciri calls *curaditos* to what others call *curados*. In Oaxaca, *curados* are usually made with *aguardiente*s that are infused with fruits and herbs for a long time. Mrs. Cirina Leyva Vera or Doña Ciri, as her friends call her, was born in Pinotepa de Don Luis. She has been preparing *curados* of up to 30 different flavors made from various fruits and herbs for forty years, which have to be aged for at least one month. "I age the *curado* for two or three years, I have a cellar, but I can't uncover them because they are aged," explains Doña Ciri, who has bitter *curados* that are aged in *aguardiente* for up to one year.

Her *curaditos* are a traditional drink she hopes to pass down to the next generation, which is why she teaches her daughter the trade. Among the herbs, plants, and roots she uses in her *curados* are: *ruda*, *coyote*, spearmint, mint, ginger, anise, *moringa*, and *huaco*.

The drinks are tasty and also have healing properties. Anise and ginger *curados* are good for digestion; the ginger *curado* is also good for a cough or a cold; the one from *coyote* is helpful for those with diabetes, to ease phlegm, for anger or for the nerves; *moringa* is for diabetics and can also be helpful for stress; *huaco curado* works as an antidepressant.

"God gives me wisdom and understanding so I can find more flavors. I named it *Curaditos Doña Ciri* because they are for healing the stomach, the throat, the head," she explains with joy.

Doña Ciri's various *curados* or *curaditos* can be found in Pinotepa de Don Luis, where everyone in town knows where her stand is located and they all know how to get there. She sells the *curaditos* in a quarter, a half, and a whole liter. They are enjoyed on their own, without food as they are for healing.

46

Atole de plátano macho

Deep inside a jungle area near Cacaluta beach, in Huatulco, there is a ranch brimming with palm trees, banana trees, and cornfields. There, Mrs. Cenorina Vázquez Sáchez —originally from Mixtepec, but has been living in Huatulco for forty-eight years— starts a fire to prepare plantain *atole*. "When I arrived here I was young. I lived in Copalita and my husband would go to La Bocana for plantains. A lady told me not to discard ripe plantains, to take advantage of them, since you could make plantain *atole* with them," recalls Mrs. Ceno. Her son-in-law, Francisco Ríos Ramírez, known as "El Grillo," picks the plantains from the trees to make *atole*.

"I stopped fishing and switched to working the fields. We've had these lands since 1984 and every eight months we have to cut a cluster from the trees. Each cluster has about 25 plantains," he explains.

Cenorina Vázquez Sánchez

Banana trees first arrived to the region a few centuries ago. Local black communities settled there during colonial times spread the use of several varieties of the plant and promoted it for its versatility, not just the fruit, but also the leaves and even the stem. One of the most delicious and popular types of bananas are plantains. Francisco cuts the clusters from the trees and lets them rest on the ground for three or four days, until they are ripe. The riper they are, the better the taste. Afterwards, Mrs. Ceno chooses the ripest plantains, washes them thoroughly and cooks them whole, peel and everything. Once boiled, she discards the boiling water and lets them cool down before peeling and mashing them with a *jícara* (drinking gourd). She then boils them again in a new batch of water. "We used to mash them by hand, with a bit of water, but it used to come out too liquid-y and *atole* has to be thick, it is better with a *jícara*," she explains while continuously stirring the *atole* using a wooden spoon, to prevent the beverage from burning.

Thanks to the double boiling, the plantains acquire a thick consistency and it is no longer necessary to strain them to achieve the right texture. The end result is delicious and sweet, even without no additional sweeteners. Today, only a few households in the area prepare this healthy drink. It is not sold in markets or stalls like most traditional drinks.

Cenorina Vázquez Sánchez

47

Atole de
tortilla quemada

As foods prepared with corn become better known, the diversity of the produce, its uses, and its possibilities multiply. Not only to sustain the body, but to relieve it, or both, which speaks of Oaxaca's culinary wisdom. An example of this is this type of *atole*. *Atole de tortilla quemada* is a delicious drink that is descriptive of its elaboration process, though not of its delicious flavor: golden, smoked, and burnt notes that Oaxacans and Mexicans in general have a taste for. "My mother used to make *atole de tortilla*," says Cenoria Vázquez Sánchez, originally from Mixtepec." "[She] browned her leftover *tostadas* and *tortillas*, browned them in a *comal*, and began placing them in a pot; I learned from my mom," she mentions as she sets a pot over the fire. It all starts with the corn *tostadas* that are intended for the drink. Once these are ready, a bit blackened over the coals, without any fat, before they are completely burnt so they have more flavor, they are placed next to the rest of the ingredients to prepare the *atole*.

The first step is placing the pot on the stove and adding some water. As it warms up, a little *panela* is added and, once diluted, cinnamon and a large, chopped tostada are added until it all boils at once. Then, all there is is looking after the drink, as it foams and can spill over or stick to the pot, so Mrs. Cenorina constantly stirs the *atole* with a wooden spoon.

Once it boils, it can be served after allowing it to cool down slightly. This drink is enjoyed both hot and cold, it all depends on the person drinking it.

"If your stomach is upset, you can make *agua de tortilla* with four *tostadas* and it cures vomiting, it is a *medicina*, it calms the pain," says Mrs. Cenorina, or Ceno, as her friends and family call her.

This isn't a commercial drink so it can't be found for sale. It is an *atole* that very few people make at home, mostly just for an upset stomach.

Juana Ramírez Gopar

48
Cocol

Cocol or *"coco loco"* ("crazy coconut") is a refreshing and traditional beverage from the Oaxacan Coast, where it is consumed to battle the heat and high temperatures of the region. It is prepared in Laguna de Chacahua, but also in Pochutla, Puerto Ángel, and Pinotepa Nacional, among other coastal towns.

In Chacahua, Juana Ramírez Gopar learned to make *cocol* thirty years ago. "I learned how to make the drink with my mom. It can be enjoyed on its own or with alcohol," says Juana while carrying three coconuts for the drink.

The coconut is a plant with a long history in tropical and subtropical regions of all continents, making its origins uncertain, though it is believed that its wild ancestor could have come from Southeast Asia or South America, which spread before it became domesticated millions of years ago.

Juana selects the coconuts and cuts them using a machete with remarkable agility. Then, she drains the fruit's water into a clay pot and extracts its flesh. Coconuts used to be crushed with a hand mill until achieving a more liquid consistency, but nowadays a blender is used for that same purpose. Juana mixes this paste with the fruit's water in a clay pot, adds spearmint, a little bit of cinnamon, and grenadine for a pinkish hue. Condensed milk can be added to make it sweeter. Once the drink is made it is recommended to keep it refrigerated to serve it cold. Some people like to add *mezcal*, aguardiente, or a 96 proof liquor, depending on their preference. If the *cocol* is meant for a patron saint party, a wedding, or another celebration, it is served on its own, with no alcohol. Sometimes up to two hundred coconuts are used for this purpose.

"Coconut has a lot of calcium, a lot of protein. My husband had a stroke and he drinks a lot of coconut and is already getting better," says Juana while serving the *cocol* inside a half coconut shell.

Hilaria Canseco

49

Champurrado chatino

Chatinos are one of the sixteen indigenous groups of Oaxaca. They live in Santos Reyes Nopala and other nearby towns, about six hours south of the state capital. They make a *champurrado* they call *Ijkua*, it is the famous Chatino *champurrado*. The word *champurrado* comes from the Spanish word *"champurrar,"* which means mixing one liquor with another, though in Mexico it defines an *atole* made with water, cocoa, and sugar. It is a very well known drink.

"My mom taught me. I would say to her, 'Mom please show me how to roast this since I don't know how to.' 'Daughter, this is how you roast, come see, I'm going to teach you, but I'll tell you just once, there's no time to ask how,' she said. I told her, 'Ok,' and that's how I learned to roast a quarter, a half a kilo," shares Mrs. Hilaria Canseco, a native of Santos Reyes Nopala, who has been making this drink for over fifty years.

To make this *champurrado*, Hilaria first secures the cocoa, cleans it by removing any debris it could have and then roasts it in a *comal* until it turns black like coal.

Hilaria toasts a bit of cinnamon until it is "golden brown," then she places the *panela* over a stone and, with another, smaller one, she grinds it until it turns to powder. She places the toasted cinnamon on a *metate* and adds cocoa to create a black paste that she transfers to a large gourd, adds a bit of *panela* and continues grinding.

At the end, she grabs a little bit with her hands and mixes the paste to make balls the size of an apple.

That same day or a day in advance of making the *champurrado*, very early, the *tlaciahual* is made, cooled, and then taken to the mill to finely grind. Once Hilaria returns with the ground corn, she brings it to a boil, stirring it with a wooden spoon.

Once boiling, she adds a bit of *panela* and one of the cocoa paste balls she had prepared beforehand. "One knows when it's good, when it's right, until it has boiled," she explains. After boiling, it's cooled down before serving in *jícaras*.

This drink is common during patron saint parties such as those for San Pedro, San Juan, or Santiaguito, for example. It is also served for a *tequio*, a communal work system such as the collective roofing of a house or cementing a floor.

50

Atole
de sapo

Atole de sapo, which literally translates to "toad *atole*," is a drink that's made in Santiago Jamiltepec and, despite its name, it does not in fact contain the amphibian. It is instead prepared with corn, *panela*, and cinnamon. The beverage is also known as *atole de masa* (corn dough *atole*) in Santa Catarina Juquila.

It is among the traditional *atoles* found in many Oaxacan communities, though with its own elaboration technique that gives it a unique flavor, consistency, and texture. "I learned from my grandmother when she used to make it about fifteen years ago. Some people in Juquila would give *atole de masa* to babies after breastfeeding instead of [milk] formula. Here in Jamiltepec it was served at parties," says Myriam Bautista Canseco, a native of Santa Catarina Juquila. After removing the kernels from the corn, the grains are brought to a boil with a bit of slaked lime, as if it were *nixtamal*. It is an important variation of the recipe as it adds a unique touch to the drink, given that the corn is not nixtamalized. "It's washed and, once washed, it is sent to the mill, and then you have *masa*, like for making *tortillas*," she explains.

Myriam Bautista Canseco

She then brings water, *panela*, and cinnamon to a boil. She places the *masa* in a different container, mixes it by hand with a bit of water, strains it with a cheesecloth to remove any lumps, and adds the liquid to the pot filled with water, *panela*, and cinnamon. As with other *atoles*, it must be constantly stirred to prevent it from sticking to the clay pot or burning. In Santa Catarina Juquila it is given to nursing children as it is believed to be nutritious, though it's a tradition that's being lost. Meanwhile, in Santiago Jamiltepec, the beverage is still served at rosary prayers or festivities, but fewer and fewer people are making it nowadays.

51

Pozol de

pixtle

Guadalupe de la Cruz Merino

In Santiago Jamiltepec there is an excellent drink called *pozol de pixtle*. It is prepared with *pixtles* (pits from the *mamey* fruit), corn, and *panela*. The *pixtle* is rich in fat, it generates foam in certain drinks and adds a pleasant taste to others. This drink, in particular, is made with the kernels of the *cacahuacintle* corn —used to make the *pozol*— which bursts open after cooking and brings to mind foam (*pozol* in Nahuatl language). Therefore, this word is assigned to beverages made with this type of corn, those who have foam or appear to have it.

Mrs. Guadalupe de la Cruz Merino, originally from Santiago Jamiltepec, has been making *pozol de pixtle* for several years, which she sells house by house in this coastal town. She learned how to prepare the drink from her aunt and her mother many years ago. Her native language is Mixtec, which is why Mrs. Miguelina Torres Salinas translated during this interview.

Pozol de pixtle can be enjoyed on a daily basis. Guadalupe buys the pits, or *pixtles*, and dries them in the sun for five months. Once dried, she must boil them twice. The first time she washes them with salt and water. She boils them again the following day, but just with water, and dries them in the sun once more for three days. Once the *mamey* pits are dried, they are ground in a *metate* along with the cooked corn and the crushed *panela*. When everything is ground, it is mixed with water, and it's ready! It has a refreshing taste. There are five or six people still preparing this beverage in Santiago Jamiltepec who go around town to sell the drink everyday.

Judith Juárez Sánchez

52
Café
Finca El Nueve

After water and tea, coffee is the most consumed beverage in the world. A good coffee is born in the countryside, at a noble plantation. A farm needs good land and good weather, which are the first conditions to plant a coffee of excellence. Oaxaca is a privileged land that has all the characteristics needed to obtain the highest quality coffee beans in the world. "I was born in a coffee plantation. I really spent all of my childhood in a coffee plantation, between coffee sacs, between coffee scores, between pinches of coffee, everything coffee. I think

that's how I started getting involved with the work they did. I inherited the love for "El Nueve" from my grandmother," says Judith Juárez Sánchez, a Pluma coffee producer for more than thirty years. Judith went to "El Nueve" during the holidays. Once there, she helped her grandmother who was in charge of coffee production. "My grandmother would tell me, "let's see, you don't have anything to do? Go grate the coffee, go pinch, go cook.' Then, I got into this coffee business," she recalls.

At the end of April and early May, the coffee plants begin to flower. After that, there are nine months to harvest. "The thing about coffee in the highest zone is that ripening takes much longer, it has a higher oil concentration, which sets the aroma more. The bean is heavier too, when you roast a coffee like this, of *altura* (height), it has less volume than when you roast a coffee from the lower zone," explains Judith.

The plantation has a nursery for germinating seeds. After six weeks, the small plants are ready to be transplanted into bags and, after one year, strong and resistant, they are introduced to the fields. They will bear fruits after four years. "We are organic, we don't fertilize using agrochemicals, but those who do have a harvest after three years, it accelerated everything," says Judith.

The harvest is thorough, tiring, and difficult due to the weather, the mosquitoes, and other insects at the plantation. Víctor Canseco López, from Santa María Huatulco, has been working at "El Nueve" for 11 years, and is currently in charge of production and maintenance of the coffee and plantation. "We harvest only ripe beans, we take the pulp out that same day with clean water from a spring that has no agents of any kind, just the natural ones from the spring, all the work is done with clean water," says Víctor.

Mostly *Typica* is planted, though *Márago, Bourbon*, and *Catuaí* are being introduced.

The fruit, or cherry, selected at "El Nueve" is only the ripe or red one. After weighing the coffee cherries, they are scattered in a pond filled with water to eliminate the lower quality beans. The ones that float usually have a single bean or are rotten. Then, they are submerged into pulping machines to remove the flesh from the drupes, leaving just the parchment coffee in a different pond.

The following day, Víctor extracts the coffee from the pond and piles it up. He overlays two sheets so the sun doesn't interfere with fermentation. Then it rests in the shade for 36 hours and, after that, it is washed so the coffee can release its honey.

After three or four days, depending on the weather, the beans are sun-dried. They are "grated" three times, meaning they are turned on both sides with a special wooden shovel until they are ready, though they are also experimenting with drying grids instead of handling the coffee by hand to avoid damaging the beans. Once the coffee is dry, it is placed inside 46-kilogram parchment sacs.

"Everything influences the quality of the coffee. If you roast it, how you store it, how you pulp it, if you pulp it at the right time, the water you use, if you don't go over the fermentation time, or you washed it ahead of time, and so on. How you dried it, if it's fully dried or if it's moist, if you didn't over dry it, etc.," explains Judith.

The *altura* (height) coffee of Café Finca "El Nueve" is sold in beans, ground, or as a cup at Café Huatulco, a cafeteria that Judith and her husband, Salvador López Toledo, have owned for more than 20 years. This café is located at Huatulco city's kiosk where, besides coffee, they also serve food such as *tamales* and a stew from the Isthmus.

Cañada

A *cañada* (ravine) is the "space of land between two heights that are not far from each other," which is what characterizes this region, the smallest of the eight that make up the territory of Oaxaca. Its highest point is 3,000 meters above sea level and the lowest is 574 meters. To the north, it shares borders with the state of Puebla and the Tuxtepec district; to the south and west with the Mixtec region and with the Etla and Ixtlán districts; and to the east with the Sierra Norte region.

The region has two prominent rivers: The Salado and the Tomellín. The first runs through the famed Tehuacán Valley of Puebla, to the north, while the Tomellín river, also called the Río Grande, brings along water from the Sierra de Ixtlán, which irrigates the south,

creating one of the most exuberant areas of Oaxaca, as it is where mangoes, melons, watermelons, limes, oranges, and *chicozapotes* are grown, along with an abundant amount of sugar cane fields.

Cañada is overflowing with beautiful and diverse flowers that allow for a wonderful honey production because of the bees found in the area. The climate is warm, which favors a diversity of plants. However, in the areas near the mountains, cacti such as the organ pipe and the Mexican giant cardon proliferate, and animals like the armadillo and possum abound in this habitat. In regards to the culinary richness of the region, it is a land full of exquisite traditional dishes —many of which are endemic to the area— as well as *aguas de sabores* (*aguas frescas* or flavored waters) and other drinks.

53

Atole agrio
de Santos
Reyes Pápalo

Raquel Silva

In the mountains near Cuicatlán locals prepare an *atole* whose roots come from ancestral and possibly pre-Hispanic times, like few other drinks found in the nation. This drink is the *atole agrio*, or sour *atole*, which can be enjoyed in Santos Reyes Pápalo.

This countryside *atole* is traditionally enjoyed with a meal that is consumed after corn harvest. The drink has a bitter and sour taste, hence its name, which brings to mind the enormous diversity and complexity of flavors that humans can enjoy, and even though it is not as dense as most *atoles*, it holds traces and the energy of corn that allows for it to be called an *atole*. Plus, it is white in color and has the inherited symbolisms linking it with the Mesoamerican worldview. To prepare the *atole agrio*, the corn kernels are cut off from the cob when it is "solid" and soaked in water overnight to soften the grains.

"This recipe belongs to the 'people of the Sierra'," says Mrs. Raquel Silva from Santos Reyes Pápalo. "Since it is a bit cold there, they place the pot next to the stove so the corn turns bitter and sour on purpose," she mentions while grinding the grains that were soaked the previous night.

Once the corn has been ground, the *masa* (dough) is strained into a clay pot with cold water, which is then brought to a boil until the liquid is ready. "The process does not have any sugar or cinnamon and the corn is not cooked," meaning it is not nixtamalized or cooked beforehand, "it is raw and ground corn," says Mrs. Raquel, who makes this delicious and comforting beverage.

The *atole* is served hot and it is not a commercial drink but one enjoyed at home, although Mrs. Raquel Silva can make it, if requested ahead of time, at the Los Arcos restaurant in Cuicatlán.

Agripina Heras

54

Curado de
zarzamora

In Oaxaca, aguardiente, just like *pulque*, can be made into *curados*. The name brings to mind those drinks which, because of their properties, can cure or heal. And in this case they were originally meant to be remedies, but because of their taste they ended up becoming a delight for the palate. About forty minutes away from Cuicatlán is Concepción Pápalo. It is a town in the mountains that's steeped in cold to cool weather most of the year. Fruits such as tejocote, apple, blackberry, and quince can be found in the region, among others. The blackberry was brought to Mexico, but it is of European and Asian origin. "I go collect them from the fields, I will cut the fruit, and when I can't go myself someone will bring them to me or I will buy them," says Agripina Heras "Pina," as her friends call her, who's originally from Concepción Pápalo and who's been making blackberry curado for over 25 years. Blackberry season goes from August to November, although Pina knows that the fruit can be found almost year-round because of the area's cold weather.

Pina collects, washes, and disinfects the fruits, then crushes them inside of a clay bowl. She then strains the blackberries into a jar, using a cheesecloth, to decant the fruit's liquid.

She adds the same amount of sugar cane *aguardiente* to the jar with the concentrated fruit juice. Sugar is also added to balance out the fruit's acidity. "The mix is allowed to rest, even though it can be enjoyed at once. The more you let it rest, the more it will age and flavors will intensify, as well as the alcohol,"

says Pina. The alcohol content can reach 35 to 45 proof, depending on aging. In addition to making blackberry *curado*, Pina makes this drink with other regional fruits such as quince, apple, and *tejocote*.

The fruits should never be boiled, just crushed or chopped to infuse the *aguardiente* with them. Ay time of the year is a good time to visit Concepción Pápalo and enjoy these *curados*. They can be bought as a liter and onwards.

55

Atole agrio

de Huautla
de Jiménez

Emma Méndez García

Fermentation is one of the most important techniques used on foods to obtain products with a certain alcohol content, especially beverages that are extraordinary because of their qualities and flavors. The sour *atole* from Huautla de Jiménez is made with fermented corn and *ayocote* beans, a large bean that grows copiously in the Cañada region. It also has a *pipián* made with *chiltepe chile* seeds and sesame seeds. Even though it is a beverage, because of its thickness it looks more like a broth or food.

"Since I was ten years old my mother would tell me to pay attention to the ingredients used, because the corn has to be prepared properly first and, once clean, it is washed and soaked for three days," says Mrs. Emma Méndez García, who's originally from Huautla de Jiménez. The corn is soaked in water and, after three days, the liquid is discarded, the conr is rinsed and then transferred to a *metate*. It can be soaked for up to four days, it just depends on personal preference.

The resulting *masa* (dough) is fermented for another night. The following day, it is strained twice, decanting it with a cheesecloth used as a strainer, to get a very smooth liquid. Then the *atole* is cooked in a clay pot. "Do not stop stirring because it will burn, and movement also adds flavor and once it's cooked it is served in a *jícara*," says Emma. At the same time, the sesame seeds and *chiltepe chile* seeds are roasted, being careful not to burn them. Then everything is ground in a *metate* and, once ground, it is mixed by hand inside of a clay container, adding water and a little bit of *masa*. The ingredients are always added in the same sequence to serve in a *jícara*. First, the *atole* is poured in, then the cooked *ayocote* beans and, finally, Mrs. Emma uses her hand to add the *pipián* on top of the drink.

Atole agrio is prepared for all kinds of events: weddings, funerals, and patron saint celebrations. Don't miss out on trying this delicacy if you visit Huautla de Jiménez.

56 Pozole

Pozole has many variations. In San Jerónimo Tecóatl, in Teotitlán del Camino, *pozole* is enjoyed as a beverage. The word *pozole* is traditionally used to refer to a type of stew that's made with *cacahuazintle* corn. It is a dish of pre-Hispanic origin that evolved into different variations, but this is not the beverage that bears the same name in San Jerónimo. "It is a drink that us farmers usually enjoy in the fields during lunchtime, which is at noon. Before eating our sacred food, we prepare our beverage, *pozole*, and drink it to cool down a bit. Then, we proceed to eat and then continue with out work routine in the fields," says Mr. Trinidad Duarte Canseco, who's originally from San Jerónimo Tecóatl, a farmer and beekeeper.

Trinidad Duarte Canseco

Pozole is made with white corn *masa* (dough), from ears Mr. Trinidad harvests each season. Once the kernels have been cut off the cob, his wife nixtamalizes and grinds them, and the resulting *masa* is wrapped in freshly cut *heliconia* (also known as lobster-claws) leaves, which she gives to her husband for lunch along with a *jícara*. "In the same way, the *tacos* that my wife and daughter prepares for us at home are wrapped in *heliconia* leaves and in a cloth napkin so they remain soft until it's time for lunch in the fields," he says. At an early age, Mr. Trinidad learned from his parents how to prepare this drink to be consumed at the fields in order to refresh and restore the mind and stomach of those who work at planting black beans, *ayocote* beans, corn, or as beekeepers —a family trade that started with his grandfather, Cristino Duarte, and his father, Memo Duarte.

Water and corn are everything. In the middle of the fields, Mr. Trinidad pulls out the *jícara*, walks to a spring near near his *milpa*, scoops a bit of water, sits on a log, opens a *heliconia* leaf and adds a bit of *masa*, mixes it with his hand, and enjoys the refreshing drink to be able to eat the food of the day. "*Pozole* is vital for us because at once it feeds us, quenches our thirst, and strengthens us because of the physical wear and tear," he concludes.

57

Calabaza

de chilacayota

Rosaura Reyes Merino

Mrs. Rosaura Reyes Merino, from San Jerónimo Tecóatl, a community within the Sierra Mazateca, prepares the *calabaza de chilacayota* (a squash, also known as fig-leaf gourd) drink thanks to her mother, Mrs. Amparito Merino, who shared this knowledge with her. The *chilacayota* is a part of the *milpa*, from the Nahuatl *milpan*, itself from *milli* "sown plot" and *pan* "on top of." Once an immense *chilacayota*, similar to a watermelon, ripens in the family *milpa*, it is picked. Rosaura cuts it in half and scrapes its insides. "It is cut with a knife and a wooden stick is used to scrape and pick to detach and tear apart all the threads, and this is done for a while," explains Mrs. Rosaura. With the help of her daughter, Marta Duarte Reyes, she rapes and picks the insides of the *chilacayota*.

Then, she heats up the flesh with a little bit of water and once it boils she scoops out the foam. At the same time, Marta cuts off the kernels from some ears of corn and chops a few others.

She places the chopped corn and the kernels along with the *chilacayota* into a pot filled with water. After three hours, she adds cinnamon and a little bit of sugar, just as it begins to boil. Mrs. Rosaura uses the hollowed out *chilacayota* as a container to mix nixtamalized *masa*. Once mixed, she and Marta strain the mixture through a cheesecloth. The *masa* is placed in the pot with the boiling water to incorporate all the flavors into a single drink. "When it acquires a light color, like beige, it means the squash is starting to cook. It is continuously stirred to prevent it from sticking," shares Mrs. Rosaura. As with other *atoles*, the stirring step is essential to prevent the drink from burning.

Once boiled, it is allowed to rest and cool down as the drink is enjoyed cold. Its consistency is curiously light, very different from other *atoles*. It is a home drink, not for sale or prepared for parties. It is only enjoyed during harvest season.

Mayra Mariscal Hernández

58

Pulque de cardón

The landscape of San Juan Bautista Cuicatlán, in the Oaxacan Cañada, is breaming with beautiful and large cacti or *cardones*. They bloom in April and May and give a purplish pink fruit covered in thorns that's called a *cardón*.

This cactus is very high and, in order to obtain its fruits, which are similar to prickly pears, it is necessary to use poles or reeds that can reach the plant's summit of up to five and ten meters high, allowing for proper pruning. They are bluish green candlesticks that look slender, as if aiming to reach the sky. The fruit is very refreshing and its juice can easily dye clothes. "To go pick this fruit you have to either go very early or very late because of the heat. We have to bring our reed to the slopes of the hill; a bucket.

And to be able to cut the fruits we bring them home, we clean and carefully, because of the many thorns, open them, and carefully remove the pulp with a spoon, which we place in a little dish," explains Mayra Mariscal Hernández, from Cuicatlán.

While the *cardones* are being cut open and their skins removed, Mayra brings water to a boil. Once it starts boiling, she immerses the fruit's pulp in the water. It is kept there for several minutes, then removed from the heat, and the liquid is transferred to another clay pot, covered, and left to ferment for three days. This *pulque* is only prepared in a clay pot, otherwise it won't properly ferment. "After those three fermentation days we strain it, because of the seeds, and add a little sugar to sweeten the drink, and if we want it cold we have to add some ice, but the ice has to be in a separate bag, otherwise the flavor becomes diluted," says Mayra, who is also a *chilhuacle chile* producer, which is one of the endemic wonders of Oaxaca. The *cardón* is a survival fruit. It is consumed in its entirety, including its seeds. In Cuicatlán, there are ladies who sell *pulque de cardón* on every season, despite the difficulty of picking the *cardón*, the tortuous extraction of the flesh because of the skin's thorns, and the seasonality of the fruit, although there are fewer traditional cooks who are preparing it nowadays.

Epifanio Cruz García

59

Café de

Santa Cruz Acatepec

Coffee trees where introduced to Oaxaca during the second half of the 19th century, when demand for cochineal decreased. It quickly became an important economic activity for many Zapotec, Chatino, Chontal, and Mixe communities in the Sierra Sur and Coast. The results were evidently good, as coffee drinking became popular and Oaxacan coffee was well liked and, since then, many farmers decided to try various types and cultivation forms to achieve optimal results. Currently, in Cañada, 27 of the 45 municipalities produce coffee, so it is one of the most important economic activities of the region, with parchment coffee —usually of the *typica* variety— being the predominant bean.

For 25 years, Mr. Epifanio Cruz García has been working on coffee production in Santa Cruz Acatepec, a community located twenty minutes away from San Jerónimo Tecóatl, on the way to Huautla de Jiménez. He likes a good cup of coffee with sugar or *piloncillo*, a beverage he enjoys on a daily basis. "I have worked with coffee since I was about fifteen years old, and that's how I learned everything about coffee, and from there I was at an organization where I worked for about 12 years, and that's where I learned about coffee," says Mr. Epifanio. He owns several plots with coffee crops, one of these, close to his home, but unlike a plantation, as the sowed area is small. "I was also changing my plants, adding other plants such as the *geisha* and other plants like *pacamaras*, *caturra*,

I have also planted some *bourbon*, *typica*, and *dessie*, which we are trying out to see the fruit and quality, says Mr. Epifanio. In Santa Cruz Acatepec the sowing starts in June, with the first rain of the season, and harvesting begins in October, when the coffee "cherries" begin to ripen, and goes on until January.

After each picking, Mr. Epifanio and his family de-pulp the coffee, wash it, and dry it in meshes to be sold as quality parchment coffee. "Well, I'm going to keep fighting and working. My daughter, my wife, they help me, and I'm also inviting my other children to make an effort with coffee. Our coffee is very good, of great quality," says Mr. Epifanio.

Gudelia Iglesias Cancino

60

Chileatole
de Concepción
Pápalo

Chileatole is a drink found in many Mexican towns, particularly in Oaxaca. Many Oaxacan communities have their own versions and people who prepare it. However, the marriage of *chile* and tender corn kernels can be surprising at times, especially if you know how to apply the appropriate techniques along with the perfect ingredients to achieve unique flavors. In Concepción Pápalo, a town located 45 minutes away from Cuicatlán, on the way to the mountain, a *chileatole* made with *chiltepe chile* is prepared. "First the corn is picked, kernels are cut off from the cobs, and then it is ground. And once it is ground, it is strained and boiled. You add a little bit of salt and a little bit of sugar, some *chile* and *epazote*," says Mrs. Gudelia Iglesias Cancino, originally from Concepción Pápalo, who learned the secret to making this drink from a very young age. Mrs. Gudelia cooks the corn in a clay pot over the fire and, once it's boiling, she

adds a touch of cinnamon to make the *atole*. Once cooked, she removes it from the heat and uses that same water to mix the *masa* she had previously ground in a *metate*. To this *chileatole*, Gudelia adds *chiltepe chile* and *epazote*. Both the *epazote* and the *chile* grow in her garden and with these ingredients she finishes seasoning the drink.

This is a seasonal drink, which can only be enjoyed during harvest season, usually in October. There are people who sell it around town, but it is usually enjoyed at home. *Chiltepe chile* and cinnamon are a unique twist that is vital to enjoy in Concepción Pápalo. The remaining corn us used to make other stews while the *chileatole* is being prepared. "This [is] also for making bean *tamales* or bean or corn *memelitas*, so this is how I make it," ends Mrs. Gudelia.

Raquel Silva Méndez

61

Licor de tejocote

Tejocotes are a well-known but not very esteemed fruit, perhaps because of its bittersweet taste. However, when sugar is added to the pulp an addicting flavor ensues, which is why demand for it hasn't decreased with time.

The word tejocote is the Spanish version of *texocotl*, which is the Nahuatl word for the same fruit. It comes from *tetl* "stone" and by extension "a hard thing," and *xocotl* "sour or sour fruit." Meaning, "sour and hard fruit".

Tejocotes, originally from Mexico, are round, fleshy, hard, sweet and sour fruits that have very hard pits, thin and smooth skin, and are yellow or orange with tiny brown spots. They are very fragrant. During the dry season, they can be found at the markets of Oaxaca and are used for *ponches*, jams, candied, and liquors. "I learned to make *licor de tejocote* with an aunt, my grandfather's sister. I was ten or twelve years old and I would go to her home to see how she prepared things," says Mrs. Raquel Silva Méndez, a traditional cook who's originally from San Juan Bautista Cuicatlán.

This liquor is prepared in November and December. During these months, Mrs. Raquel buys the fruits, chops them into small pieces and dries them. For this, she places the small pieces of fruit on aluminum trays, then arranges the trays around her home's yard and waits between eight and fifteen days for the fruit to dehydrate in the sun. The number of days will depend on the weather. Once the *tejocotes* are dried, they are roasted in an *anafre* over a *comal*. "The *tejocotes* that grow around here in the Sierra have more flavor," she says as she moves the fruit around the griddle with a wooden spoon. Then she removes the *comal* from the *anafre* and places a clay pot filled with water in its place, adds cinnamon, processed apricot, raisins, and the roasted *tejocotes*. Sugar is added once the concoction starts to boil, which results in a syrupy consistency.

"You have to wait several hours for the syrup or tea to be cold," she explains as she removes the pot from the *anafre*.

Once it's cooled down, she scoops the liquid with a clay cup and filters it using a very thin white cloth to remove any residue. Finally, she transfers the liquid to a glass jar and adds 96 proof alcohol (drinkable). *Licor de tejocote* has only one third of alcohol.

"It has to be left to rest for about two months so it tastes well. It is prepared in December and by January or February it will be properly processed and fermented with the fruit that was added," says Mrs. Raquel. This pleasant drink can be found at Los Arcos restaurant, located in Cuicatlán.

Mixteca

The Mixteca region of Oaxaca borders to the north with the state of Puebla, to the south with the Sierra Sur region, to the east with the Sierra Norte and Central Valleys regions, and to the west with the state of Guerrero. It is a land of ravines where remains of marine fossils can be found along with caves, waterfalls of extraordinary beauty, crystal clear streams, and mountains of soft peaks. It's the home of the famous Apoala cave, in Nochixtlán, which contains a huge lagoon in one of its galleries. The most prominent river in the area is the Río Verde, which changes names as it progresses, and even though the Mixteca appears to be a poor area with scarce crops resulting from widespread erosion, it actually hides important mineral wealth with large deposits of antimony, zinc, lead, silver, gold, tungsten, manganese, iron, and mercury. Corn, beans, potatoes, rice, *chile*, and various fruits are planted on the slopes and valleys that can be cultivated, while *alfalfa* and many other grains such as wheat, barley, and fava beans are planted in the Nochixtlán Valley along with fruits such as apricot, *tejocote*, and *capulín*. The region's physical environment is diverse, as it goes from arid and semi-desert to forested and steppe, which is why its landscapes can range from beautiful organ cacti to gorgeous palm trees, resulting in a huge diversity of ecosystems with magnificent options to create beverages that compliment the regional dishes.

62

Bebidas espirituosas

Othón Jesús Valle Jiménez

Mexican herbalism is one of the most sophisticated and culturally profound reflections of our indigenous peoples' wisdom. In the nineteenth century, in 1865, at the heart of the Heroic City of Tlaxiaco, Oaxaca, the La Parroquia apothecary was founded. It is one of those rare jewels of times past since, during the first third of the twentieth century, apothecaries were turned into pharmacies by presidential decree when laboratories selling patent medicines emerged. Thus, where formerly there were cabinets full of substances to make medical prescriptions, there are now boxes with pills and syrups to cover the needs of traditional medicine. However, La Parroquia prevailed. "Here the apothecary is a vital part of the city's history, because it was the place where people were cure," explains Othón Jesus Valle Jiménez —grandson of Mr. Nicolás Jiménez, the original founder— who is now in charge of the business. La Parroquia is still preparing spiritual beverages that function as medicinal alternatives based on the "spirit of the plant," hence the name. The compounds, tinctures, and macerated products processed in the apothecary contain the natural properties of their sources. One of the advantages of these elixirs is that the body quickly absorbs them because of the alcohol they contain. "Depending on the plant, the properties can be extracted from the root, the stem, the leaf, the fruit, or the flower," says Othón while he arranges some herbs at the apothecary's counter. Each plant —*coyote, arnica, huaco, valeriana, ruda, pericón,* anise, *cedrón, flor de tila,* ginger, and *itamorreal*— has a specific sowing and harvesting time, on which its properties depend.

Thirty-five years ago, Othón learned how to prepare these drinks from his parents and grandparents. The process to extract the components is simple, but it involves thorough and deep knowledge of the plant's anatomy, their selection, and the precise amounts required for each preparation. "It is a tradition here. People have been getting cured with plants for a long time. The people from these communities have even more faith in them than in pills or patent medicine, because plants are more readily available and they are also cheaper," adds Othón. First, the part of the plant that is needed for a particular remedy is acquired. Then, it is sun-dried. Drying times depend on the weather. If it is cloudy or it can take up to a month. If a root is being used, it is cut into small pieces so it can be consistently dry inside and out. Once the plant is dry, it is placed inside of a glass container filled with alcohol or aguardiente to macerate. This step also depends on the type of plant, as some release their properties faster than others. Maceration takes between one and two months. "These plants lose their properties in plastic, so they must be places inside of dark glass away from the sun," says Othón.

In Tlaxiaco and other nearby towns, people consume these medicinal beverages a lot, many of which are the legacy of pre-Hispanic times. Each person demands their plant and knows what their spiritual drink is, because there are some plants that can cure the same illness or help getting rid of similar symptoms, so the choice depends on personal taste since the flavors are varied: sweet, bitter, spicy, or even earthy.

63

Pulque de
Nochixtlán

Between twelve and fifteen years have to go by for a *pulque* maguey from Nochixtlán, in the Oaxacan Mixtec region, to reach full maturity so its *aguamiel* can be extracted, which will become *pulque* after fermentation —a drink that has come to be considered medicinal. The word *pulque* comes from *poliuhqui* or *puliuhqui*, which means "decomposed." It was how a "decomposed" *octli*, which become "corrupted" after 24 or 36 hours, was called, as it became an *octli poliuhqui*; that is, it became a "decomposed wine." Spaniards thought it was a generic word for the drink, instead of a characteristic description of it, and so the Spanish version for it became *pulque*. Of course, it does not mean that the drink is rotten, but rather that it is no longer fresh or new.

The town of Santa María Apazco is where the majority of *pulque* production in Nochixtlán takes place, which is why, in this countryside landscape, the bright, red colored soil contrasts with the fleshy green tones of the *pulque* magueys, ranging in height between twenty centimeters to almost three meters.

The Milenary Women Organization

Aguamiel extraction is complex, which is why a ritual performed in front of the plant has to be performed beforehand. Permission is requested so the plant's thorns don't harm the *tlachiquero* or *tlachiquera* who will be extracting the liquid and so it releases a good amount of *aguamiel*. "This ritual references the Virgin of Juquila a lot, who is also the Virgin of Remedies, as the plant is considered a woman, and she is a woman who constantly produces *aguamiel*, which is a reference to milk," explains Bibiana Bautista Gaytán, who's originally from Nochixtlán and currently works as a promoter for the Millenary Women Organization.

Once permission's been asked, the person prays and crosses himself, as per ancestral tradition. The men prepare the *maguey* and remove the thorns from the *pencas* (leaves), they open the heart or core of the plant and leave a hole so the women can then scrape it to collect the *aguamiel*.

Once the plant has been cleaned and a hole has been made into its heart, ten to fifteen days must go by for it to begin producing *aguamiel*. "It is not very sweet at first, but after twenty days it becomes abundant. When it's abundant, the scraping becomes constant. Once in the morning and once in the afternoon. The *aguamiel* is collected and [the plant] is scraped with a metal scraper, gently and not too deep," explains Alejandra Rodríguez, a *pulque* producer.

Among the tools used are a knife for preparation, the metal scraper (used daily to scrape the plant's heart), the *acocote* (a type of gourd used to extract the *aguamiel* through suction), and a pitcher or jug, into which the *aguamiel* is poured.

Aguamiel production is gradual, given that the maguey progressively releases its sap until it becomes abundant. The process takes between five to six months. After the extraction process, the *aguamiel* is brought to the tinacal (a sort of cellar), into the barrels, poured in with the nana. "The nana is the bitter *pulque* of a different person that has a good flavor, it's a characteristic maguey and people look for it, it's like the mother *pulque*," explains Reyna Hernández, who is part of the Millenary Women Organization. Previously, in the community, when there was no "mother *pulque*," they would look for "angel grass" (Calliandra houstoniana) leaves —a bitter plant that would help make the *aguamiel* bitter. "*Pulque* production in the region has a legend of its own, its origin is marked on the Mixtec codices, where *pulque* was used as a spiritual or ceremonial drink, when only the gods or greats priests would drink it," concludes Lucía López, a *pulque* producer.

María Rosario Ortiz

64
65
66

Ticunchi, Ticunchi
rosa y verde

To Mixtecs, *ticunchi* is the *papalometl maguey*, whose name comes from the Nahuatl papalotl "butterfly," and *metl* "maguey." It is the region's own *cupreata* agave. It is also the name given to three beverages made with this maguey in Tlaxiaco: the *ticunchi,* the pink *ticunchi*, and the green *ticunchi*. Although the word *maguey* is the Caribbean term for the plant, Mixtecs have the word *yavi* for the *agaves*. For one, the Greek word agave refers to "admirable" or "noble," and it is the nomenclature that the Swedish naturalist, Carl von Linneo, used to scientifically define this plant family that, because of its characteristics, seemed "admirable" to him. There are currently about 200 hundred *agave* species, all of them in the American continent, half of them from Mexico, among which is the agave *yavi ticunchi,* a favorite in the Mixteca region. "I have always bought the *magueyes*. It's just *papalometl*. It has to be this way, when it's already solid, when it has a *quiote* or is about to have a *quiote*," says María Rosario Ortiz, originally from Cañada Candelaria, Cuquila, who has been making this drink for twelve years. María begins preparation by collecting clover or *socoyul* leaves, along with their flowers, whose taste is sweet and acidic. María washes and rinses these *quelites*, chops them, and places them in a pot. She cleans the *maguey*, removes the *pencas* (leaves) careful not to prick herself with the thorns, and uses the white parts. She chops the plant into pieces, washes, and places these pieces into a clay pot along with the clover leaves in layers —first the clover, then the *pencas*, and so on. She turns on the stove and places the pot on top, pours some water into it, and brings it to a boil for about two hours. After boiling, María removes the juice from the plants and transfers it to a different container to cool down. From this, she gets about 30 liters that slowly turn pink because of the clovers.

With that she concludes the first drink, *ticunchi*, a drink that is only made during the rainy season, from June to September, as that is when the *socoyul* is available in the region. The second drink is made by keeping the clay pot boiling until all the properties are extracted from the plants. "Well, the *maguey* does have many medicinal properties. Here we use it for wounds, especially wounds, or for fractures, or when one is suffering from back pain. The *maguey* is very good. We already eat the *socoyul*, similar to *cilantro*, as a vegetable, that's how we eat it." This herbs replaces the tomato to make *salsas* with *chiles*. The beverage is served in a *jícara*. As for the green *ticunchi*, the reserved leaves are cooked.

"I prepare it with the *pencas*, with the maguey *pencas* and that's where the green comes from," says María, who removes the thorns from the *pencas*, washes and cuts them into small pieces, and grinds them in the *metate* to mix with the green *ticunchi*. "This one has to be enjoyed in small quantities, only a little bit, one cannot drink too much of it otherwise the person's blood pressure will go down, meaning, it lowers your pressure.

It is good for someone who suffers from high blood pressure because it helps them lower it," she says. The green *ticunchi* is a drink that's usually enjoyed on an empty stomach, and only a maximum of about two ounces since *itamorreal* can make the throat itchy if it is consumed in large quantities.

On Saturdays, plaza day, María Rosario Ortiz begins selling the drink at 7 in the morning in the Tlaxiaco market, in front of the Escuela Licenciado Pérez Gazga.

278

Ixchel Ornelas Hernández

67

Atole de
maíz

In the Heroic City of Tlaxiaco, *atole de maíz* can be made with various types of corn, though the most popular one is white corn. "This *atole* is very representative for the Mixteca and for all of Oaxaca, where there is corn there is corn *atole*," says Ixchel Ornelas Hernández, chef at the place. "Today, at the market, you can find prepared crushed corn, which allows you to bring it home with you and do the corresponding soaking to make the *atole*," says Ixchel, who cooks and researches Mixtec cuisine. "I was taught that soaking the corn kernels a day in advance allows the grain to absorb all the moisture during those twelve to twenty-four hours and then it's easier to grind in the hand mill. It needs to be a coarse grind to have some of the little pieces of the corn kernels in the *atole*. Then the corn softens and it is easier to remove the skin," says Ixchel in her restaurant's kitchen. Once the corn is ground, it is hand-mixed to completely remove the remaining skins. Then it is ground once again using a tighter disk to extract all the starch. "Starch is the part that will go to the bottom and will allow the *atole* to thicken at the end. It is a very similar process to the one used to make the corn dessert of *nicuatole*, exactly the same process actually, the only difference is the crushing of the corn," she explains. With the ground corn and the skins removed, Ixchel boils the whole thing in a clay pot over low heat. About two liters of water are added for every kilo of corn. Nothing besides the corn and the kernels are used in a white *atole*, although cinnamon, *panela*, or sugar can be added if desired. It is boiled for fifteen more minutes, stirring constantly so it doesn't stick and takes the perfect thick consistency. To promote regional corn, Ixchel uses them to make *atoles*. "One of the most important things is to highlight that the process and technique are the same, even though the flavor changes because of the corn, it's a subtle change, but yellow corn is a little bit sweeter, white corn tends to be a bit neutral, but between blue and red there is a flavor difference from the minerals, they have different flavors," she says. *Atole de maíz* can be enjoyed warm on any day of the year at home and also at local restaurants such as El Patio, in downtown Tlaxiaco, where Ixchel is chef owner.

Maricela Pérez García &
The España-García Family

68

Café Kússend

"Since my husband and I moved to Ojo de Agua, we started planting *cuajinicuil* trees among other fruit trees, whose trees serve to fertilize the soil. Time went by, we realized they produced shade and we planted coffee trees," says Rosa Regina García Feria, from the Ojo de Agua plantation, located in the town of Guadalupe Miramar, in the Tlaxiaco district. Guadalupe Miramar is one of the towns within the Santa María Yucuhiti municipality, in the Mixteca Alta, located at 1,400 and 1,900 meters above sea level, two hours away from the Heroic City of Tlaxiaco. The town is in the mountains, steeped in humid and cool weather, near the coffee growing area where *Bourbon* and heirloom *Typica* varieties grow. Every season, the coffee trees give beans that more or less mark certain notes of flavor in a cup, which can be accentuated or diluted depending on the process the beans are subjected to. Harvesting season in the area begins in October and ends in February, which encourages the the start of the cycle towards the cup. "At first, we started with the traditional washing, a process that involves collecting mature beans, de-pulping them, fermenting them for 24 hours, washing and drying them in the sun for approximately seven days, depending on the weather," explains Maricela Pérez García, founder of Kú55end —which is how the Kú55end brand is registered, "Aroma that transforms Love"—and Mrs. Rosa's and Fidel España's niece. "I went to several workshops with producers who work with differentiated coffees, in various processes that are well known in Oaxaca, to train and share this experience with the family. They were implemented and were very popular, so I gave myself the task of training my producers, my uncles, the España-García family, and my sister Elia Pérez

García, and fortunately they accepted my proposal, which meant relearning," recalls Maricela, who started the Kú55end brand, which uses the high quality beans that her family harvests. The brand does their bean selection by hand, although they used to harvest "evenly," no matter what the the plant looked like, but once they started implementing these methods to improve quality, they began pruning just the red or ripe fruits, between 22 and 26 degrees Brix, which indicates high levels of sweetness. Depending on the time, fermentation, as with other fruits, intensifies flavors. "We just leave all the skin on, we currently have many unprocessed ones with various types of fermentation, ranging from 48 to 72 hours and up to 120 days," says Maricela. Once the coffee has been de-pulped, that is, after removing its skin, it is placed in a sorting machine that selects size, then the unripe beans are manually removed, because they would otherwise affect the flavor of the finalized coffee cup, and then they decide whether they want to sell the beans green or roasted. The España-García family has the luxury of being able to do unimaginable training for many baristas, roasting masters, or producers. For example, with a freshly harvested coffee of the *enmielado* type, fermented for 72 hours, Mrs. Regina begins roasting in a *comal*, stirring constantly to avoid burning, carefully achieving an artisanal medium roast throughout. Once roasted, she grinds it in a *metate* and, at the same time, brings a clay pot filled with water to a boil, immerses the freshly ground beans, and the resulting beverage is of an unusual flavor, unlike any other type of coffee made with more recognized methods. This result can only be enjoyed at Kú55end.

Olga Cabrera Oropeza

69

Atole de trigo

Along with rice and corn, wheat is a very important cereal in the world. Egyptian and Iraqi archeologists are still fighting about the grain's paternity. The Spaniards brought the grain to Mexico, however, because of corn's prevalence in the area, it was not successful for centuries. The natives were forced to grow it to make bread and wafers, which were so important to the Hispanic diet and for the rituals of the catholic church. "It is traditional in the Mixteca region, in the towns of Nochixtlán, Tamazulápam, and Tejúpam, where wheat *atole* and *tortillas* are consumed," says Olga Cabrera Oropeza, a cook who's originally from Huajuapam de León. At the age of thirteen, Olga ventured into the world of cooking, when she helped her grandmother make various homemade dishes. That's when she learned about the different types of *atoles*, including *atole de trigo*. The cereal is collected. "It's a similar process to corn, harvesting time arrives where the what ears are picked, beaten, and passed through a sieve to sift the wheat," says

Olga. Once the wheat has been cleaned, it is ground in a hand mill several times, until it takes the consistency of flour and broken wheat, which thickens the *atole*. "Well, it is not like corn that quickly thickens just by breaking it a little bit, wheat is a lot more work," she says while grinding the grain in the *metate*, as it was done in the past. At the same time, Olga boils some water with cinnamon in a clay pot. "The flour is hydrated so lumps don't form in the hot water, or everything can be mixed at once, from cold water and bring to a boil. You have to stir it constantly so it doesn't stick and it properly thickens. My grandmother always said that when you check the *atole* to see if it's ready, it shouldn't sound like water, it has a sound of its own," says the Mixtec cook. Olga got her start in Oaxaca City with a small, four-table restaurant 17 years ago. Today, she has three restaurants where she showcases her region's cuisine, where one can enjoy *atole de trigo*.

One of those restaurants was proposed by the

Oaxacan singer Lila Downs. "Five years ago, I get a visit from the singer Lila Downs, on a Sunday, which was the only day I has Mixtec food. That day I had *pozole*, *chilate*, *guachimole*, and it caught her attention. She asked why I made Mixtec food and I told her it's because I'm from the Mixteca, she liked it a lot. Soon she came back and proposed we opened a restaurant here, at her mother's home," she recalls.

"My thing and what I know how to make is my region's food, I was a bit closed off, but fortunately we've done very well, we have this restaurant, the restaurant in the Centro Histórico, and the small restaurant; I've had the opportunity to travel to other states and abroad to present Mixtec food, and today I can say I don't regret being stubborn and saying that I am Mixtec and I want Mixtec food to be known and valued," she concludes. *Atole de trigo* is a beverage that can be enjoyed hot or cold on a daily basis, though it is generally served hot for breakfast.

Istmo

It is one of the narrowest areas of Mexico. It occupies 18% of the territory of Oaxaca and, because of its size, it is the second most important region of the state. To the north, it borders with the state of Veracruz, to the east with the state of Chiapas, to the west with the Sierra Norte and the Sierra Madre del Sur and, to the south, with the Pacific Ocean. Its landscape is filled with mountains, plains, and coasts. To the north, the Tehuantepec Valley is framed by the Sierra Atravesada and the Ixtaltepec mountains. The south has a coastal hem along the Pacific. Since its lands are at sea level, there are many salt water lagoons in the area. The east abounds with plains and strong winds. In the Sierra Atravesada, the Sun and Moon mountains are separated by a pit that forms into a canyon of high cliffs, under which the Zanatepec River runs. The tributaries of the Coatzcacoalcos River emanate from the Sierra Atravesada. Within the Gulf of Tehuantepec lies the Laguna de Marqués, famous for its salt production.

The Salina Cruz harbor is an oil port, but it also has a major shrimp fleet to capture the crustacean used to make *pozol del Istmo*. The Bahía de la Ventosa is also a part of this region, as is the long coastal lagoon known as the Dead Sea. Most of the soil covering the Tehuantepec Valley is alluvial and its tropical climate boosts fertility. There are bountiful forests in the mountains, to the north and east, and mangroves and swamps along the coast. East of the Tehuantepec River there's a wide fringe of tall palm trees and mango, orange, and avocado trees thriving.

70

Chileatole
del Istmo

Florina Manuel López

Chileatole is a common drink in indigenous Mexican communities that are strongly linked with the *milpa*. It is an energetic *atole* with several iterations, whose preparation techniques are as varied as the corn and *chile* types used depending on local wisdom.

Although it may appear more of a "meal" that's similar to *esquites* or *pozole*, because of its texture, consistency, flavor, and purpose, it is definitely a beverage. In this case, white corn and *chile piquín* are used for its preparation.

This is Florina Manuel López's, or Dulce's —as her friends call her— variation, which has made her famous in her community. Although she is a native of Juchitán, she has been living in Asunción Ixtaltepec for many years. "An aunt taught me fifteen years ago," she says; and she's been keeping the tradition alive since then.

In order to make it, Dulce selects the corn ears at the market. She starts at five in the morning since she makes large quantities. First, she removes the *totomoxtle* (husk) from the corn and cuts the kernels off from the cob. Then she divides the grains into two, some for the *tamales* and some for the *atole*. "Then I begin cooking the corn," she says, "I peel about eighty or one hundred ears of corn." According to her recipe, she reuses the water where she cooked the corn, so she reserves the liquid. Meanwhile, she grinds the selected corn for the *atole* using a hand mill. Then she strains the resulting *masa* (dough) with a cheesecloth and brings it to a boil in a pot. At the same time, she grinds the green *chile piquín* with a bit of water in a *molcajete*.

Finally, to serve the drink, the *salsa* is added to the *atole* to achieve the desired flavors. The result is spectacular as the *salsa's* spiciness is combined with the *atole's* sweetness. The *chileatole* —which ends up not being too thick, unlike a regular *atole*— is served in *jícaras*. It is garnished with *epazote* and some corn, and can be enjoyed alongside *tamalaes*, though not necessarily.

In addition to the *chileatole*, Dulce makes corn *tamales* and weaves *huipiles* (she embroidered the *huipil* shown in the photographs herself). If you wish to try this *chileatole del Istmo*, you have to go to Asunción Ixtaltepec and ask for her at the banks of the irrigation channel 33, in the Second Section of the Santa Rita neighborhood.

Francisca Rasgado Vázquez

71

Bu'pu

The main, shared characteristic among the many traditional Mexican beverages made with cocoa is their lavish foam. The most famous is hot chocolate, but there are several other drinks enjoyed in Oaxaca that, unlike their famed sister, maintain that sophisticated and special peculiarity, one of which is *bu'pu*.

Bu'pu is a Zapotec word that means "cocoa foam". It is a traditional drink from the Isthmus region that is served in *jícaras* or glasses overflowing with foam — hence its name— delighting all those who drink it.

Francisca Rasgado Vázquez has been making this traditional drink for the past seven years. She was born in Juchitán de Zaragoza. "It is a drink that should not be misses, it is a traditional drink and that is why I am pleased to make it, to share it so people know about it," says Francisca about *bu'pu*. "It is good for the health and it is made with natural flowers," she adds while placing the ingredients on a table.

Similar to many other drinks, the first step is to light the wood burning stove until the wood reaches the right temperature, over which she places a pan to roast the cocoa. The beans are stirred around using a wooden spoon until they are evenly browned. She repeats this step with the fresh flowers of *guiecha'chi'* or "may flower," *guiebacua*, and *guiexhoba*. The roasted ingredients are then allowed to rest.

Then, Francisca makes the "*piloncillo* sand," for which she places a blanket on the floor and, over it, she places some *piloncillo* bars, wraps them up and, using a rolling pin, she crushes them forcefully. The *piloncillo* has to be processed "until it is broken, until it becomes sand and dust," Francisca says with a smile as she lifts the ten-kilogram rolling pin and hits the blanket with it. The *piloncillo* sand is ready an hour and a half later.

Once the *piloncillo* sand is ready, Francisca grinds the cocoa and adds the flowers and a little cinnamon to it, "I add a little bit of water and I get this paste. I have to place this paste in the freezer, otherwise it will be watery and it won't make a lot of foam," she explains.

In addition to the liquid cocoa paste, a corn *atole* must be prepared to make the *bu'pu*. For this, a pot filled with water and corn is placed over the fire. "After it's been coked I have to bring it to the mill, meanwhile the stove stays on, I return with the corn and start straining it," she explains.

With a very thin and fine mesh, she strains the *masa* and decants it to remove any skins. The filtered liquid is brought to a boil in a different pot until it a sort of film forms on top. "When the *atole*, as it is now, is boiling, I strain it once again to remove that film." She does this everyday so she can offer a fresh drink of exceptional flavor.

As for the making of the *bu'pu*, two pots are used: a clay one, to which she adds only cold water and the foam producing cocoa paste, and an aluminum one that holds the corn *atole*. "I keep it warm and when it starts to cool I have my *anafre* and coal and I heat it up," says Francisca.

Bu'pu is served hot. First, the *atole* is poured into a *jícara*, which comes from a tree called *morro*. Then, after five minutes of whisking the cocoa paste, the foam is placed on top of the *atole*.

In the Isthmus, this traditional drink is usually made for various celebrations, including weddings, baptisms, masses, or wedding proposals. It can also be enjoyed in the afternoon after 6 any day of the week in front of Juchitán's Municipal Palace, right next to the market. There, Francisca and other women sell this sophisticated drink.

72

Ni Xiaba Nidxi

(atole con leche)

Rosa Elba Antonio Ortiz

Among the many beverages of Oaxaca, there are some that stand out because they are so closely linked to their rituals, among which is *Ni Xiaba Nidxi*, which is the Zapotec name for an *atole* with milk.

It is a peculiar drink because it is ritualistic. It is related to the times of The Viceroyalty of New Spain, because it is made with milk, sugar, and cinnamon. In the Isthmus, it is traditional to drink it for Day of the Dead, or All Saints' Day, as well as at wakes. "It is the drink they make at night with a *tamal*, it is offered to people, and also for prayer or at mass," says Rosa Elba Antonio Ortiz, who learned how to make this *atole* —that in Asunción Ixtaltepec has a special flavor— with her grandmother.

To start, Rosy cooks the corn until it softens. Once the corn is ready, it is ground in a hand mill. "The corn has to be strained first to remove all the skins. I find it easier to add some water before straining it, so it's better strained, because if it all goes inside the pot it will be too watery," says Rosy as she strains the corn. Then, she adds some water to the clay pot so it starts boiling. It is important to keep an eye on the pot; it is the most delicate step to prevent the *atole* from sticking. Once the *atole* thickens, Rosy adds milk, a cinnamon stick —which floats on its surface— and a little bit of sugar to sweeten it.

The perfect complement to this hot drink can be a beef *tamal*.

73
Taberna

When the *coyul* tree reaches maturity, it can be cut down to obtain its sap and, with it, prepare a traditional Isthmenian drink. "The drink is called *taberna*, we know it as the ancestral drink of the Zapotecs," says José Luis Toledo Morales, from Unión Hidalgo, who has been working on *taberna* production for over 35 years. At six in the morning, before the day warms up, José Luis selects the palm tree and, using a machete and an ax, he begins pruning the tree, carefully avoiding its thorns. On the tall tree stem, he carves and punctures a square of about 20 centimeters. The hole is made behind the area where the bud blooms, which is where its core can be found, an essential step because the plant can rot if it's not done correctly. "It is important to scrape it well, to make a good hole and clean it daily, you have to remove all the bark that dries everyday to allow the new bark to release the sap to make water again," the man explains. The hole is covered with a leaf from the same palm tree and a stone is placed on top to prevent animals from sucking the liquid. "The process continues two or three days after the drilling with very sweet and clear water that, in this town, is used as a healing drink, while fasting, for people with kidney stones, they drink it and it helps removing the stones. The sweet water process takes a week, and after the second week it starts fermenting and the flavor becomes stronger," says José Luis. If the palm tree is large, three extractions can be made daily: at six in the morning, at one and at seven in the afternoon. If it is not extracted, the sap will spill over. Then, it is stored in 40 to 45 liter barrels and allowed to ferment for up to twenty days. The piece of the plant that was extracted from the hole is submerged inside the barrel to accelerate fermentation. "After this time, we can consume a strong tasting fermented *taberna*," says José Luis, who belongs to the third generation of *taberna* producers in his family. *Taberna* is enjoyed two different ways: on its own, with its strong fermented flavor, or diluted with water, ice, and sugar. There are two production seasons in the Isthmus: Holy Week and All Saint's Day. "It is tradition in town to celebrate the dead with an altar and the traditional drink is *agua de taberna*, which is shared with the guests that come visit the altars. During this season, about 400 to 500 liters are made".

José Luis Toledo Morales

Sustainability is important to José Luis, therefore, he plants five or six palm trees for every one he cuts down, with the goal that future generations can also enjoy this drink. "It is an endangered drink because of its laborious process; you have to cut down the tree, which is a tree completely full of thorns, you have to be experienced in maneuvering it. You have to know how to work the plant, bring it down carefully, remove as many thorns as possible because these thorns, when they cut into your skin, they move quickly through your veins and it's a very though and resistant thorn that moves through a person's skin and can sometimes stay inside the human body, which hurts a lot," says José Luis.

You will have to travel to Unión Hidalgo to enjoy this drink. You can find José Luis on Calle Benito Juárez 16, Centro. "All those who want to try *taberna* can come visit, it will be a pleasure taking care of them," he concludes.

Dora Luz de la Cruz Toledo

74

Pozol del Istmo

This drink, considered a *pozol*, is made with the *nixtamal* of *cacahuazintle* corn popped in flower. "*Pozol* is a Zapotec drink that is consumed in different parts of the state. In this community, it is traditional to enjoy it along with food," explains Dora Luz de la Cruz Toledo, from Unión Hidalgo. The *nixtamal* is ground using a hand mill or *metate*. The ground *masa* (dough) is shaped into a ball and placed inside of a *jícara* with water and it is mixed by hand or with a whisk until the dough dissolves. Dora and her cousin, Nuria Betsabé Díaz Toledo, do this work. Her cousin is a cook who, like herself, learned how to make her mother's, aunts', and grandmothers' dishes from a very young age, keeping the traditions and ancestral wisdom of Oaxacan cooking alive. The water used must be cold, so the drink is refreshing. In the Isthmus, this *pozol* is usually served with dried shrimp from the region, although there is also the option to enjoy it with sugar or *panela*. *Pozol* is a piece of Zapotec food, it is enjoyed at parties, commemorations, or simply on a hot day, it is very common in this area of Oaxaca. "The *masa* to make *pozol* as well as the drink are still sold at the market," says Dora. It is both a drink and a food.

Papaloapan

This region is located northeast of the Sierra de Oaxaca or Sierra Norte. Its name comes from its ties with the Papaloapan River, which irrigates a good part of the territory and it is also a reason for the hot and humid climate of the region. Comprising over 11% of the state's territory, the Papaloapam region is also one of the richest areas of Oaxaca because of the diversity of products found in the area as well as its soil fertility. It is also known by the name of "Tuxtepec region". In regards to borders, to the north and east it neighbors with the state of Veracruz, to the south and west with the Sierra de Oaxaca, and to the southeast with the Isthmus.

75

Atole
de pataxte

Cecilia Ángeles Jiménez

Arroyo de Banco is a town located within the San Juan Bautista Valle Nacional municipality, in the Tuxtepec district —part of the Chinantla cultural area— where the exquisite *atole de pataxte* is made, which is only prepared for the Day of the Dead or Faithful Dead celebrations, in late October and early November. "At the age of twelve, I saw how my mother prepared this cocoa. We were looking for it in the mountain. It is common to find it in Arroyo de Banco. Yes, family's make it, they prepare it, they don't sell it. Younger people today don't like it because they prefer sodas than the traditional regional drink," says Cecilia Ángeles Jiménez, originally from Arroyo de Banco. To make *atole de pataxte*, Cecilia goes out to collect the white cocoa, finds and washes its seeds. "The seeds are washed as if they were coffee beans, inside of a basket, and then they are sun-dried for several days, it is a slow process," says Cecilia. Once the *pataxte* is dry, it is roasted in a *comal* until its shell is slightly blackened. The roasted beans are then crushed with a stone over a wooden table, one by one, to remove their shells. "This process is slow and tiring. You have to be patient," says Cecilia. Meanwhile, she nixtamalizes the corn, without boiling the grains, so they remain a bit crisp. She mixes and grinds it in a *metate* along with the shelled *pataxte*, adding some toasted cinnamon to this. "To prepare the *atole*, water is poured into a pot and then you add the *masa*, or *pataxte* paste, which has been ground in the *metate* with a bit of sugar and honey." The Chinanteca community of Arroyo de Banco is in the mountains, where the weather ranges from cool to cold with a bit of humidity, so the clouds and fog can be seen far below. This weather is perfect for drinking a hot *atole de pataxte*, apart from the fact that because of the fat the cocoa releases, it cannot be enjoyed cold. It is an *atole* that comforts the body with its warmth, which is maybe why it is served for the Day of the Dead celebrations.

Juana Jerónimo Hernández

76

Pozol blanco

Pozol is a traditional drink from the states of Tabasco, Chiapas, and Oaxaca. However, the one from San Juan Bautista Valle Nacional not only differs from those of the first two states, but also from those of other Oaxacan towns, which makes it an emblematic *pozol* of the Papaloapan Basin and of the Tuxtepec district. "You learn how to make it as a child because that's what all the moms make, so one learns to make it," says Juana Jerónimo Hernández, originally from Valle Nacional, who was taught as a child how to make the drink. Corn selection is very important, and it has to be a dry corn. Juana goes to her *milpa* to pick some ears of corn, she cuts the kernels off, and cleans the corn to make the *nixtamal*. This technique is a reflection of the ancestral wisdom that knew how to make the grain more easily digestible and increase its nutritional value. Nixtamalization is linked to the type of corn being used, since each one takes a different amount of time and knowing the exact time is an art, as it is linked with the final product desired, whether it is *atole*, *tortillas*, *masa*, *masa* to make *tostadas*, or *pozol*. Once the grain boils, it is removed from the pot and she waits for it to cool down to wash it. "It has to be refrigerated properly so all the skins can be removed, all the husks, and once the corn is well washed, it is cooked over the fire once again until the corn pops," explains Juana. Juana grinds the popped corn, gradually obtaining a paste, which she places in a *jícara* with water and whisks it using a small *molinillo*, to be able to enjoy a refreshing drink. Either sugar or honey can be added to *pozol blanco*, although honey is a bit more common because of the large local production of this sweetener. *Pozol* is an everyday drink. It is nutritious and very refreshing for those who are struggling with hot weather like that of the Papaloapan Basin.